IT'S IMPOSSIBLE TO START A FIRE

4315-ELLI

IT'S IMPOSSIBLE TO START A FIRE

If You Have No Desire To Burn

Jeff Ellis

To order additional copies of this book, contact:
Xlibris Corporation
1-888-7-XLIBRIS
www.Xlibris.com
Orders@Xlibris.com

CONTENTS

He was a pudgy little sophomore. I was an upperclassman. According to my friends who did know him, Jeremy was one of those kids you would see hanging out behind the school, puffing on a cigarette and falling off their skateboards. I was Vice President of the Speech and Debate Club. I wore a suit to school every Friday and spent my weekends at tournaments across Dallas. We might as well have been going to different schools.

It happened on Tuesday, at the beginning of second period. I was in my theater class. We used to meet in the auditorium and would spend most of the class hanging out on the stage, ignoring our well-meaning but ineffectual teacher. Fifteen minutes into class, the screaming started.

It came from out in the hall. A girl screaming, "NO! NO! NO!" A girl screaming in the hallway of a high school; nothing unusual. We laughed it off. But the screaming didn't stop. "NO! NO! NO!" Slowly, we all realized something was truly wrong. Something had actually happened.

"HE'S DEAD!" the girl screamed.

Our teacher ran out to the hall and most of the class followed. As for me, I stayed seated on the stage. I was trying to ignore it all. That's the way I handled problems back then. Sometimes, it's the way I handle them now. One of the students – his name was Brad and he'd be dead himself in the Persian Gulf within the upcoming year – walked back into the room and said, "Some kid shot himself."

"What?" I replied. He had to be joking.

"Some sophomore shot himself," Brad repeated. His voice was so matter-of-fact that I can still hear its blandness. How should he have said it? How do you say something like that without sounding strange?

Our teacher ordered the rest of the class back into the auditorium. He told us to get off the stage and sit out in the audience section. Our principal, Mr. Bishop, herded Jeremy Delle's former classmates into the auditorium and told them to sit on the stage and wait. As if they were sheep, they silently did as told.

JEFFREY'S SPOKEN

I have been trying to tell Jeremy's story for a decade now.

Jeremy Wade Delle. You may not know the name but if you've listened to FM radio any time since 1992, then you've heard a musician's rendering of Jeremy Wade Delle. If you've watched MTV, you've seen a filmmaker's vision of Jeremy Wade Delle. Jeremy is the deceased teen martyred by Pearl Jam in the song of the same name. He is the inspiration for that music video that, a few years back, won all those awards.

However, before Jeremy Wade Delle could become a part of pop culture, he had to walk into my old English classroom at Richardson High School, put a gun to his head, and pull the trigger.

In the final months of 1990, he did just that.

I was seventeen years old.

Ever since it happened, people have asked me, "Did you know him?"

There was a time when I would lie and say yes. I used to skip classes with him. I used to joke with him. Sometimes, he seemed somewhat sad but certainly never suicidal. By killing himself in a public school at the age of 15, Jeremy became the type of legend that I spent my entire youth dreaming of being. While I was trying to establish some sort of persona for myself by sending out stories and poems, Jeremy was a household name. By claiming to know him, I was trying to steal a little bit of his legend for my own.

The truth of the matter was that I never met Jeremy Delle probably passed him in the hall several times during that sem ter but I would never have been able to pick him out of a line

They sat up there on stage; a numb collection of lost children. My class watched them as if we were just sitting through a rather somber play and those numb children were just actors. Some of them were crying. Despite later rumors, no one was splattered with Jeremy's blood. Most of them just had the same blank, stunned look on their face. I saw some people I knew. There was the girl that I'd been flirting with since the 8th grade. A year later, I'd ask her to prom just to discover that my best friend had beat me to the punch. Another one of them would be my debate partner during my senior year. Later, I found out they'd all been in Mrs. Barnett's Sophomore English class. Mrs. Barnett was my former teacher. Once she told my mother, "Though Jeff's grades don't reflect it, he is a brilliant student." It was one of the few times during my teen years (or any years after that) when I was truly happy.

But for now, all that was important was that every one of these people had just seen some kid blow his brains out. One of my classmates decided to play counselor. He went over them (probably humming *Kumbaya* in his head) and told them to start talking, to express their feelings. No one said anything as Mr. Bishop led him away.

A few minutes later, we heard the sirens of approaching ambulances and police and it was then that I finally had my first real reaction. I felt something sinking deep into the pit of my stomach as it registered that those sirens were coming to take a dead body out of my old English classroom. A couple of police officers came into the auditorium to talk to the witnesses. The rest of us were sent upstairs to the main drama classroom; the Studio we used to call it in an attempt to bring some Warholian glitz to our little department.

We stayed in the Studio for two hours, waiting for some word. We split into small, informal "discussion" groups. Some sat in circles and cried. Some wondered which of the school's many Jeremys had killed himself. And my group? There were six of us and after we decided that school would probably be can-

celled for the rest of the day, we made plans to catch a movie. I
know that sounds awfully cold on our parts. Maybe that was our
way of coping. Or maybe that's just the way we really were. I
can't remember for sure.

After two hours, Mr. Bishop came over the speakers and
announced a student had shot himself. He didn't give the name.
Instead, he announced that this was tragedy. And he encouraged
us to stay out of the way of the cops. Finally, he said that he had
spent the last few hours debating whether to cancel the rest of
the day's classes. We all held our breaths, hoping to hear the words
of freedom.

Instead, Mr. Bishop said, "However, canceling classes will
not change what has happened. As soon as the bell rings, please
go to your next regularly scheduled class."

Everyone groaned. We still had to go to class!? Why were we
being punished!? After all, we hadn't shot ourselves in front of
crowded classroom.

What were the reactions that day? It is true that there were a
few seniors who wandered around saying, "Leave it to a sopho-
more." One of my best friends was sick that day and later, he
bitterly remarked, "The first time something interesting hap-
pens at school and I miss it!" Others ran around with tears stream-
ing down their faces, talking about how life was a "dark journey"
and all that other trendy young nihilism. Most of the school,
though, was just stunned. Stunned and silent.

I went to the rest of my classes but no one bothered to teach
that day. Some teachers talked of tragedy and others just asked
(begged really) us to entertain ourselves. In my creative writing
class, an aspiring poetess named Julia told me I was heartless when
I complained about not getting to go home early. We then ate
lunch together and spent the whole time discussing *Heathers,* a
relatively new film at that time. We wondered if this would start
a new trend at Richardson High School of students shooting
themselves in English class. Who would be next we wondered? A

cheerleader maybe? How about a jock? No, probably not. They had everything to live for. It'd probably be the blue-haired boy who claimed he was bisexual. Or maybe the pregnant white trash girl who said *ratt* instead of *right*. Oh, I was affected by the tragedy of it all now. Either that or else it was Julia's thick brown hair and long, shapely legs. But something was getting to me. At least until my next class.

After the final school bell rang, I went by the Speech and Debate room. We had a meeting scheduled for that afternoon. Our coach asked if I thought we should actually still have the meeting. "He wasn't a member of Speech and Debate, was he?" I replied.

Again, maybe that was just my way of coping. Or maybe I really was just that cold and heartless. I can't really remember for sure. After all, it was a couple of years ago.

Jeremy Delle made the national news and for a week, there were several urgent, breathless reports about depressed kids with guns. There were rumors about why Jeremy had killed himself but the few people who had actually known him didn't think he'd been any more depressed than usual. His parents were divorced and he lived with his father who some claimed was a drunk who used to beat his son like some sort of Dickensian monster. I saw Mr. Delle on the news after his son's death and he looked no worse than anyone else's father.

As for Richardson High School, life got back to normal. They kept Mrs. Barnett's classroom closed and boarded up for the rest of the year and occasionally, someone would randomly break into tears. The counselors remained active to help the distraught. However, the rest of us had classes to attend. There was a rumor that school would be cancelled so all of us strangers could go to Jeremy's funeral and maybe catch a movie afterward, but it didn't happen.

A year later, I first decided to write a story about Jeremy Delle. At first, I was going to write in the voice of Jeremy but then I realized I wasn't suicidal and couldn't really relate. So, I decided to write about the school's reaction. I was going to write about that day; or more honestly, what that day should have been like. In my story, you wouldn't find me dismissing Jeremy's death as a way to get out of school early. You wouldn't hear me asking, "He wasn't a member of Speech and Debate, was he?" No, in my story, you'd find Charles Abraham Wax, sensitive writer dealing with human tragedy.

One day, after school, I was sitting out in the courtyard where I had eaten lunch with Julia and talked about *Heathers*. I had my notebook and I was jotting down everything I could remember about that day. Stephanie, an old friend of mine (I'd known her for two years which, in the hurly-burly world of high school, made her an old friend), walked out to the courtyard and asked me what I was doing.

"Writing a story about Jeremy Delle," I said, "I'm trying to remember everything that happened that day."

"The entire school was so quiet," she said, "for the next two weeks. Nobody said anything."

I didn't remember the silence lasting quite that long but I wrote her words down anyway. Stephanie was cute and I wasn't going to argue with her memories.

Suddenly, she said, "Why do you want to write about that? People are just now getting over it."

That caught me off guard. "I thought everyone was over it."

"They're not," she said.

I never did write that story.

When Pearl Jam's *Jeremy* first showed up on the radio, I was a community college freshman. I can't tell you exactly when I first heard it. All I know is that whenever I turned on the radio in the dying months of 1992, I heard the sound of Pearl Jam's oh-so-tortured lead singer, Eddie Vedder, intoning, "Jeremy spoke in class today." I knew the song was based on a true story of teen suicide but for some reason, I never made the connection. Even now, a part of me finds it impossible to believe that a bunch of guys in Seattle built their fame on a guy I went to high school with.

The truth about the song was revealed to me in October when I was appearing in a school play. Twenty young Texans were cast as Cockneys in turn-of-the-century England. It was a comedy, a murder mystery, a social drama, and best forgotten. One night, in between acts, I was bonding with two other actors, Sean and Josh, over a pack of cigarettes. Josh asked me where I'd graduated from.

"Richardson High School," I replied.

Sean grinned and started to sing, "Jeremy spoke in class today . . ."

"What?" I said.

"That happened at your school, dude," Josh replied.

Sean asked me if I had known Jeremy. And yes, I certainly did. I used to smoke with him. It was really a bummer when he died, I'd explain with a sad shrug, but it had to happen some day. Sean and Josh were properly impressed.

By January of 1993, I had transferred to the University of North Texas. Higher Education had never been one of the major goals of my life and my sole reason for going to UNT was to hang out with my then-girlfriend, Jordan (not her real name). One night, we were watching MTV. The properly bland VJ announced that the next video would be, "Pearl Jam's *Jeremy*."

I watched in quiet fury. On TV, a thin, dark-haired twerp who couldn't have been any older than 12 sat in an impersonal, white classroom that looked like something out of a Kubrick film. This wasn't the classroom where I'd been a "brilliant student." I watched as other children, even younger than this *faux*Jeremy, pointed, laughed, and pushed him towards suicide. They all wore what appeared to be private school uniforms – white shirts, plaid skirts, dark slacks. In the world of Pearl Jam, the Catholic Church apparently ran my high school. Part of me knew that this video was meant to be a reflection of the song and not reality. But as I listened to Eddie Vedder declare that Jeremy had spoken in class today, I could only think of the innocents who couldn't bring themselves to speak after he splattered his brains over Mrs. Barnett's walls.

The video was over in six minutes. It took six minutes to martyr Jeremy Delle and turn him into some symbol for alienated Generation X. It took six minutes to tell the rest of the world that his blood was on the hands of a girl I wanted to take to prom and of a boy who later became my debate partner. It took six minutes to recreate the truth into something with a good beat. You could sing along to the tragedy.

I turned to Jordan and I told her, half-jokingly, that once I was a famous whatever, "I'm going to track down Eddie Vedder and kick his whiny Seattle ass."

A few months later, Eddie came to me and about a thousand other students. Pearl Jam was touring to promote its new CD. One of their stops would be UNT and it seemed the entire campus, myself included, was swept up in Vedder fever. No matter how much I hated that video, Eddie was a superstar and he was coming to my college.

Tickets were sold in the Student Union. Jordan and I were amongst the hundreds who camped outside to get the best seats. As we waited for the Union to open, all talk centered around Eddie Vedder. About how Eddie truly cared about his fans. About how Eddie was so deep and complex. About how Eddie could walk on water. We debated who would win in a fight, Eddie or Kurt Cobain? We agreed it was no contest. Eddie all the way. Why? I think because he was coming to UNT.

Inevitably, the talk came around to Jeremy. Everyone seemed to know somebody who committed suicide. And I do mean everyone. It was almost as if a dead friend was the newest fashion accessory. I found myself wondering if perhaps our fellow students had specifically gone out of their way to befriend the most depressed people they could find just to make sure they had a fair shot of notching up at least one suicide-related trauma.

Everyone knew a Jeremy. However, as I proudly informed them, I knew the Jeremy.

"Whoaaaa!" came the replies, "Really?"

Yeah, I told them. I knew him. I repeated what I'd confided to Josh, Sean, and so many others. I had it down to an art. Everyone was properly impressed. Everyone except for Jordan.

After we had gotten the tickets, she asked me if I'd really known Jeremy Delle. Now, this was my girlfriend. This was Jordan and I loved her in my narcissistic, immature way. I couldn't lie to her. But I couldn't bring myself to tell her the truth either. Instead, I just shrugged.

"Do you remember what you said after you saw the video?" she asked.

Again, I didn't want to tell the truth. So I just shrugged again and let the conversation end.

Pearl Jam arrived three months later. They played in the Coliseum; the same place where graduates got their diplomas and where UNT's basketball team lost every game like clockwork. More people came to see Eddie Vedder than ever attended graduation or a game. Sitting with Jordan near the hastily constructed stage, I was awed by the crowd. Frat boys, dopers, computer geeks, Young Republicans, militant activists; they had all come to see Eddie. In the back of my mind, I knew they had all heard about Jeremy Delle and didn't have the slightest idea who he was.

And neither did I.

My thoughts were interrupted by the opening act, the Butthole Surfers. As one of the greatest Texas bands ever played, a small mosh pit formed at the base of the stage. However, most of the crowd watched in respectful boredom as the Surfers set their drums on fire and an old episode of *Charlie's Angels* played on a screen behind the stage. As the Surfers left the stage, a chant started to ring through the Coliseum. "WE WANT EDDIE! WE WANT EDDIE!" *NO! NO! NO!* "WE WANT EDDIE! WE WANT EDDIE!" *HE'S DEAD!* "WE WANT EDDIE!"

When Eddie Vedder and Pearl Jam did step onto the stage, the roar from the crowd crashed down like a wave of adulation. Eddie responded by giving us the finger. As he tore into the first song, half the audience jumped from their seats and went for the stage. The pounding of their feet nearly drowned out Eddie's musical angst.

After the first song, he stared out at us and, as all Yankees feel the need to do, he said, "Deep in the heart of Texas." Then, in a voice full of contempt, he asked, "So, how does it feel to be rich?" Someone in the audience shouted back, "You tell us, Eddie!" My response was more to the tune of, "Pretty fucking great!"

Eddie proceeded to inform us that it was Kurt Vonnegut's birthday. Behind me, a girl with a gleaming nosering asked, "Who?" Still, when Eddie led us in singing *Happy Birthday*, the girl enthusiastically joined in. Eddie assured us that "Kurt" would be sent a tape of our birthday greetings. I'm sure Mr. Vonnegut appreciated it just as I'm sure Billy Pilgrim remains unstuck in time.

After the relatively cheerful sing along, Eddie's face reverted to its usual look of loathing and he started to spastically pace the stage as the rest of the band started into the musical intro of – could it be? Yes! Yes, it was! *JEREMY!* The crowd cheered at the familiar chords as Eddie told us how clearly he could remember picking on the boy and he had seemed to be only a harmless little shit until Jeremy spoke in class that day. The shaky angst of his voice may have been stolen from *Teenage Wasteland* and his shaky movements were little more than Joe Cocker with better hair but Eddie Vedder did have a presence. That night, on our stage, he was the most charismatic rip-off artist in the world. On that stage, Eddie Vedder, Seattle Rock God, became every disenchanted young Texan.

In the mosh pit, greedy hands were holding aloft a young

woman. She had long blonde hair and was wearing blue jeans and white tank top. The hands supporting her were groping at her breasts and grabbing her crotch. Strangers were violating her but she didn't seem to care or even notice. Her face was enraptured with Eddie and her arms reached out to him in a desperate invitation. Eddie stood on stage, oblivious to her, his body shaking with theatrical rage as he screamed out that Jeremy had spoken.

As I watched that girl begging for the rock star's blessing, I realized that Jeremy hadn't spoken. Jeremy had died. Jeremy walked into a classroom and shot himself without a word. Eddie Vedder was the only one speaking. Eddie Vedder and me.

At that moment, the thing only I could feel was absolute hatred for all three of us. Jeremy had died so I could have a story. Jeremy died so Eddie could give the fingers to his fans. Jeremy, Eddie, and me – the Holy Trinity of Liars.

I was deaf for three days after the concert. To be honest, I got over my hatred once the next song began. When Eddie started to sing that he'd rather be with an animal, I was dancing along with everyone else. However, after the concert, I would never again claim Jeremy's friendship.

A lot has changed since then. Grunge music ran its course. Eddie Vedder and Pearl Jam no longer rule the radio airwaves. After we finally broke up for the final time, Jordan went to England and married a far better man than me. Julia writes esoteric articles about nude photography. I occasionally run into Sean and Josh in Dallas. We talk about theater but never very long because we've run out of stories to tell. Jeremy Delle never comes up. I live far from UNT. My memories of high school are slowly fading. Even the day Jeremy Delle killed himself isn't as clear as it once was and I know very soon, this story is the only thing I'll have to remind me that it happened at all.

A few months after Pearl Jam played UNT, Kurt Cobain proved all us Eddie Vedder fans wrong by finally defeating his upstart rival. Kurt killed himself. How could Eddie top that? Kurt shot himself in the head, just like Jeremy. Suddenly, everyone had a new martyr. Jeremy was no longer needed. He's forgotten. His song shows up occasionally on the radio but now its angst has been replaced with nostalgia. He serves as a quaint reminder of a time when we could say the world was evil, we were good, and there was no need to worry about the complexities of reality.

I used to tell myself that I was going to write the true story of Jeremy Wade Delle. I was going to be the one to set Eddie Vedder straight. But the truth of the matter is that I don't know Jeremy Delle's story. All I know is that one day, he walked into my old English classroom and shot himself.

The rest is invention.

JULY 5TH, 2001

Got a charming e-mail from Jessica Evans or Adams or whatever (who, from now on, I think I should just call "my ex"), the gist of which was that I am an "arrogant, self-centered, narcissist." She ended with, "Charlie, do the world a favor and grow up!" I wanted to reply that that *is* the problem. I did grow up and this is who I turned out to be. Instead, I simply typed "Goodbye," and clicked on send. I probably should have asked her where she was writing from. Considered sending her another e-mail to ask but I know, as always, her account will probably be closed before she even gets my first reply.

THE VILE PERFUME OF BLAZING BREAD

Hell, I won't deny it was a good-looking toaster. It was a silver box. I know that doesn't sound like much but if you'd seen your reflection in its bright plating, you'd have thought it was beautiful.

Until you got to know the damn thing.

It was a Christmas present from some guy in Alabama who once dated my sister, Beth. Apparently, he made household appliances for a living. Being a casually apathetic writer, I looked down at the toaster, smirked, and said, "Can't have enough of those."

The next Saturday found me at my computer, working on the Great American Novel (a.k.a. my excuse for taking a semester off and moving in with Beth and her terminally stupid husband, Jake). I had managed to write one hundred and thirty-two pages and as I began chapter two, my mind was blocked. I stared into the blue screen until it transformed into a rolling tide – the words floating across as if they were fish in the ocean.

Finally, near midnight, I went to the kitchen to get a drink. Looking in the refrigerator, I discovered Beth had failed, again, to go to the store. Frustrated, I slammed my open palms down on the countertop and that's when it happened. I caught my reflection in the toaster.

Like a preteen first discovering pornography, I stared at the image, this contorted, grotesque image of me. In the twisted reflection, my chin stuck far from my face, like some cartoon character having his lower lip used as a slingshot. My forehead loomed high into the ceiling and my cheeks collapsed into my face, making me look like some hollowed out alien from a Steven Spielberg movie.

It was weird but my God it was beautiful.

Concepts started to flood my mind. Characterization, plot, fancy turns of the phrase – all the crap I'd always defensively cursed as superfluous in my creative writing classes! Suddenly, I possessed that power, the holy miracle of inspiration. Staring at my reflection – familiar yet undiscovered – I knew what Dante must have felt when he first set eyes on his Beatrice. Until three in the morning, I wrote.

Over the next two months, I produced over two hundred pages. Whenever I ran into a creative block, I went into the kitchen and stared at the image in the toaster. I still had no concept to what all of this writing would ultimately add up but Hell, I had three hundred and fifty pages! Finally, I knew the time was right to begin chapter three.

And then, one night, things went terribly wrong. We had all just finished dinner and I was staring at my reflection in the toaster.

"Hey," Jake suddenly said, "we haven't used the toaster yet."

"You're right," Beth agreed, "we haven't."

"I have," I muttered.

Jake wandered over to the pantry, got a piece of bread, and roughly jammed it into my toaster.

BWOOP!

What a strange, unholy sound! At first, I couldn't believe my toaster was making that sound.

Silence.

Silence.

Silence.

Silence.

Silence.

POP!

The smoking bread leapt out of the toaster. Jake grabbed the toast and jammed it into his mouth. Loudly chewing like some idiotic Faulknerian man-child, he nodded his approval.

My toaster. Jake had violated my toaster!

The vile odor of burnt bread hung in the air like radioactive fallout. It was a terrible, indescribable stench – yeast doused with rancid sewer water is the closest I dare come. The stink penetrated my mind, wiping clean any thoughts I dared have.

I sat in front of my computer for the rest of the night. The smell lingered in the air and in my mind, it formed into a solid writer's block. Foolishly, I entered the kitchen to look at my reflection but that Hellish emanation proved too strong. I ran from the toaster and to my bed where I slept a sleep filled with images of dark and foreboding things.

A week later, I again tried to write. An idea had started to form, like a gift from a Greek muse, without the help of the toaster. Suddenly, I heard someone in the kitchen.

BWOOOP!

I had to get the idea down before the whole house was filled with that toaster fragrance!

Silence.

I tried to think.

Silence.

My hands nervously hung above the keyboard, prepared to strike.

Silence.

Okay, the idea was there.

Silence.

My fingers started to come down on the keys.

POP!

That vile perfume of blazing bread jackhammered into my brain, shattering the idea. As my brother-in-law wandered through the house, noisily chewing his crispy toast, I turned off the computer. All my heroes – Poe, Fitzgerald, Kerouac, and the rest – lost their creativity to alcohol. When I dropped out of school to write my novel, I swore I'd resist all alcoholic temptation. Little had I suspected that my own personal demon rum would be married to my sister and named Jake. My hopes for reaching chapter three became a cruelly dim hope, like a rapidly fading oasis in the desert.

That night, I went to Beth and explained the problem to her. After she laughed off the perfectly reasonable suggestion of divorce, I begged her to get rid of that toaster. "For all our sakes!"

She stared at me for a minute and briefly, I allowed myself to believe that she might actually be sympathetic to my plight.

"Y'know, Charlie" my sister said, "this is just like you."

"Huh?"

"Selfish. Very selfish. We need that toaster. Every midnight, Jake gets his toast and comes back in the mood for loving."

"Beth, I can't write!"

"Oh please."

"I'm being serious."

"This conversation is over."

I went down to the kitchen and fought my way through wave after wave of that sickening aroma. I walked with my mouth open, careful not to inhale through my nose. As I moved closer to the counter, I considered Beth's words. Just as that toaster once inspired me to write, it apparently ignited Jake's sex drive. My writer's block existed so Jake could screw my sister. By the time I somehow reached the toaster, my mind felt very disturbed.

Staring at my reflection, I pushed all thoughts of sex and breathing out of my head and took in the image. My chin and the counter became one while my forehead throbbed as if my brain was about explode. My eyes, mouth, nose, every facial feature – it was all twisted, swimming in some distorted vision.

An idea.

The opening line of chapter three started to form in that pulsating forehead of mine.

It still worked! Despite all of its evil, the toaster still worked! *Praise God Almighty!* I silently cheered as I thrust a clenched fist of victory into the polluted air, *it still works!*

And in my joy, without even realizing it, I sniffed.

What's truly scary is that I felt it. I actually felt that toaster forcing its way into my head and beating the opening line to unrecognizable pulp. And that's when I knew, much like Charles Bukowski rejecting straight society for his own drunken vision, I had no choice but to sacrifice Jake's libido for my art. As I grabbed the toaster, the plug was severed from its socket in a flurry of sparks. I spent the night digging a grave in the back yard. I put the horrid thing in the ground and buried it alive.

It was a perfect crime. No witnesses. No body. Only Beth knew how I felt towards the toaster but I knew she'd never turn in her baby brother.

The next morning, Beth shook me awake and announced, "We've been robbed!"

"What?"

"We've been robbed! They only took the toaster!"

I sat up in bed, trying to look shocked. Perfect. We had been robbed.

Jake called the cops who blamed the whole thing on teenagers smoking marijuana. As Officer Trilby, the cop on the scene, explained it, "Why else would someone break into a house and only take a toaster? It's the munchies."

"Yeah," Jake responded, trying vainly to sound tough as his virility slipped away, "those bastards!"

After Trilby left, I walked outside to the toaster's grave. I stared down at the fresh earth and thought about what I'd done. It was an act of brutality but the ends justified the means or so I liked to believe. As I stood there, I felt a sudden wave of unexpected guilt.

That guilt went away as soon as I came up with the opening line of chapter three.

Hell, I won't deny it was a good-looking microwave.

APRIL 18TH, 2001

Last night, before going to bed, I got hit by this incredible need to just read something at random, so I grabbed one of those paperbacks that I bought nearly ten years back when I thought owning the right books would make me an artist. The book turned out to be *Play it As It Lays*, the first novel by Joan Didion. I'd heard good things about both. Read the novel in about two hours. It was a minimalist look at soulless people in the Hollywood of the early '70s and I hated it. Hated it like I have never hated anything before. Doesn't anyone in these minimalist, postmodern, state-of-the-world crap-a-thons ever just laugh or ever have conversations not full of foreboding foreshadowing!? Do they ever just have a good time or is that too frivolous for the serious artist? Anyway, after I feel asleep I had a dream where Joan Didion and Joyce Carol Oates visited me. Didion was in tears and quite upset with me. Oates didn't say much. Apparently, she was just there for moral support. Anyway, Didion wanted to know why I hated her book and I explained to her, in a much more polite way, the problems I had with her first novel.

"Well, who do you like!?" Didion goes, "Huh? Who does it for you, Mr. Book Expert!?"

So, I told her. Phillip Roth and Tom Wolfe.

She started laughing and as she walked out of my room, she gave me the finger.

"Is she going to be okay?" I asked Joyce Carol Oates, who I've had a huge crush on ever since I saw her picture in *The New Yorker*.

"Oh, fuck off, Charlie Wax," Oates replied, "No wonder your girlfriend hates you."

HOW I LET ALLEN GINSBERG BEAT ME OFF

I'm sitting drinking coffee
Pretending to have what other's lack
Pretending to be hooked on smack
Pretending to be talented
Pretending to be troubled
Pretending to be blessed
Pretending to be doomed

I'm dreaming in the coffee
Wishing I was illegally reading Henry Miller
With Neal Cassady
Wishing I was lost in some unknown land
With Paul and Jane Bowles
Wishing I was attending Joan's funeral
With Jack Kerouac
Wishing I was sharing a needle
With Bill Burroughs
Wishing I was smoking dope
With Gregory Corso
Wishing I was jerking off
With Allen Ginsberg

I'm living on the road
I'm eating a naked lunch
I'm heeding a distant howl
I'm looking to the sheltering sky
I'm suffering from subterranean blues
I'm holding the ticket that exploded
I'm sitting drinking coffee

NOVEMBER 13TH, 1991

After today's Milton Seminar ended (still bored out of my skull with it – all that theology and bitterness mixed in with all of those awful, awful jokes! Even Satan's a fucking bore!), went across the street to the State Club. Had lunch with Abdil, an Iranian that I know from class. Abdil started to compare Milton's theories to Yeats with his things falling apart. In order to shut him up, I told him America had entered a state of *ennui.* "Divine boredom," I explained. He liked that although I had no idea what I was talking about. Abdil decided he's bored – divinely so. I said, "Some people theorize themselves out of existence." He agreed with that too; started quoting Pascal while I had a few more beers and thought about spending the upcoming Saturday in bed with Jessica, watching cartoons.

LIVE! FROM DEATH ROW

Glory Hole, TX – What do ten homicidal lunatics and an electric chair affectionately known as "Son of Ol' Sparky" have in common? They are the stars of what many critics are already predicting will be the breakout hit of the current television season – *Live! From Death Row.*

Filmed at Glory Hole State Prison, the new "reality" show will follow ten inmates on death row over the course of the next three months. Every other week, the inmates will nominate two of their prisonmates to be executed. Viewers will then have the opportunity to vote for the prisoner they would most like to see go. The final inmate left will have the option of either having his sentence commuted to life or a cash prize of $25,000.

The show premiered two weeks ago to strong ratings and already fan favorites have emerged. By far the most popular contestant would appear to be Jimmy Boyd, a shy farm boy with a shock of red hair and an imaginary friend named Capt. Howdy. According to one anonymous Internet message, "He's definitely more Ted Bundy than Charles Manson."

While several contenders have emerged for the title of least popular inmate, the early favorite would appear to be Luther Bernerd, convicted of killing the town of Pointsford, Oklahoma. Many critics feel Bernerd lost viewer sympathy by refusing to join the prison recycling program. As well, Bernerd stunned many last week when he nominated his former cellmate, Kabu Trua, for execution. Trua, a self-proclaimed "revolutionary journalist," was executed at the end of this week's show and had been a favorite of California viewers. At press time, Las Vegas bookies were listing Bernerd as 5-2 favorite for nomination and execution.

Producer James Serpha, best known for his previous reality blockbuster *Drying Out: Lost in the Betty Ford Center*, is quick to point out, "The show has a serious message. Kids don't kill because prison isn't cool."

Serpha is currently taking applications for the show's second season.

JUNE 10TH, 1996

Been a while since I've been able to update this journal and I guess I should explain why I'm scribbling this down in Longmont, Colorado where I've been hiding out for the past week but I'm going to have to keep it quick. I came here via Greyhound; a three day ride from Dallas so I could attend the First Annual Longmont Performance Art Festival and now I know I shouldn't be here. I only realized this earlier today as I was sitting in the Longmont Elks Club, watching a transvestite sing the *Love Boat Theme* while this audience of sour looking artistes (all the men have uncombed beards, all the women speak in muted monotone – can't tell anyone apart) all discussed how they wanted to tax the rich *and* be artistically free as if they were the bastard offspring of some drunken one night stand between Karl Marx and Ayn Rand. I listen to them dropping words like Dada and Derrida and talking about the Earth as if it were some sick cousin and I realized that me, with my *National Review* subscription and my childhood fantasy of being Ronald Reagan's secret son, I do not belong here. I am a sham, a fake, a liar, a sell-out, and I react to that by drinking a lot of whiskey and smoking too many cigarettes.

Found out about this gathering via e-mail from Eddie Jinx, who edits *The Paper*, the in-house magazine of the Dallas Arts Scene. So, I caught a bus down here to see some Dallas folks take the stage but they're all apparently stranded in Colorado Springs with a dead car. So, I was the only current Texan to attend the Longmont Performance Arts Festival and the only person to come from out of town so therefore, the organizers spent a lot of time doting on me. When I was the only person in the audience, they kept asking me if Dallas was as bad as they had heard and I smiled and shrugged, feeling very shy. Watched the aforementioned transvestite. Met the group's leader – a friendly white haired man who calls himself Rik Viper. Met a cool poet named Val Ludes who told me, "I hate Dallas but I'll read there if you guys can find an audience." Everyone hates Dallas. Still bitter about JFK? Eventually, a DJ from Germany played a little techno and, drunk by now, I danced a little. An audience showed up – the bearded ones – to hear a filmmaker that calls himself Joe Criswell give a lecture. Joe's from Dallas originally but assured everyone that he hated the city and people clapped. He told us he went by the name Joe Criswell because, "I hate the real J.C.," and everyone applauded joyfully. Open mic came but I didn't read my poetry and instead sat there, drinking and listening to people with names like Veronica Breadbox (nobody seems to use their real name; your narcissistic narrator cannot comprehend this) read poems that seem to be Allen Ginsberg by way of Maya Angelou and the gene pools do not mix.

Finally, meet a girl whose name I hear but ignore and she offers to show me around nearby Boulder. We wander across the University of Colorado campus, eat ice cream, buy a biography of Marlon Brando. We go back to her apartment, have vaguely good sex (mostly because she gets on top and gives my back a rest), and I realize I won't be able to tell Jessica much about this trip. Fell asleep, woke up, and this girl was standing naked at her open window, illuminated only by moonlight and it was so much like a movie that I hoped it was. Finally, I asked her, "What are you thinking about?" She replies, monotone and flat-voiced, "I'm contemplating the dead of Denver." I start to ask what the Hell that means until I realize it's supposed to be profound. Its not but why deviate from the script now?

RICH

Rich Gulliver was my roommate during my first semester at Blazing Plain University. The college, itself, isn't important. If I had been at Harvard, Princeton, or maybe Oxford on a Rhodes Scholarship, it would be something worth going into. However, this was just a small, podunk university in west Texas with too many jocks, even more pretentious musicians with goat-tees, and a really kickass Art Department which is why I was there. Not that I was an art major (though I would be for a few weeks in the semesters yet to come) – no, I was a drama major. However, my girlfriend, Jessica, was an art major. Jessica had come to BPU for the Art Department and I had come for her.

But Rich. Rich is the story.

I guess it was a month before I was scheduled to leave the safety of my father's home that the letter arrived. The envelope had a sickly greenish hue like everything BPU sent out (we were the Mean Green Falcons, you see). Inside the envelope was a curt note informing me that I would be living in Montgomery Hall (the "artistic" dorm, as it was known). My roommate would be one Richard X. Gulliver. The letter gave me his phone number and address and strongly suggested I give him a call before moving into my room.

Well, I thought about calling him. I really did. Each day, I would wake up and give some serious consideration to calling Richard X. Gulliver. I honestly did want to know what the "X" stood for. But, I didn't call. Truth is, I didn't want a roommate. I didn't want to share my room, my stuff, or my life with anyone except for Jessica (who had been given a private room at Sapwood Hall, the all female dorm. Sapwood was better known as the Best Little Whorehouse in Texas on certain parts of the campus.)

Three days before I was scheduled to move in, the phone rang. I sat down beside my blinking answering machine, listened to my greeting message, and waited to discover who was calling.

A deep but hoarse voice came over the machine.

"Uh, hey, this is Rich Gulliver calling for . . . uh, Charles Wax is what is says on my letter—"

Quickly, I snatched up the receiver.

"Yeah, this is Charlie."

"Oh hey – uh, I'm living with you next semester."

"Yeah, I got the letter."

"Yeah."

"Yeah."

And so began one of the most awkward conversations I have ever engaged in. Both sides offered a litany of incomplete thoughts, bad jokes, and silent pauses that seemed to last for mini-eternities. He told me he rode a motorcycle. I wondered aloud where I had misplaced my driver's license. He told me he was asthmatic and couldn't handle cigarette smoke in the room. I lied and said that was kosher with me. He told me that this was his third semester as an incoming freshman and he hoped he wouldn't have to drop out this time. I decided not to pursue the matter and instead mentioned that I was a drama major. Luckily, he couldn't see the sneer that came to my face when he said he had been involved in technical theater in high school. At some point, I made a weak joke about nymphomaniacal sorority girls and he laughed a hoarse, strained bray that went on far too long to be genuine.

"Well," I finally said after fifteen minutes of this painful banter, "it was good hearing from you, Richard—"

"Uh, I prefer Rich."

"Oh. Okay, Rich."

"Yeah."

"Yeah, right, okay. Well, I'll see you later then."

"Sure thing, man."

"Bye."

"Bye."

"Oh, Rich, I just thought of something I was meaning to ask you."

His voice was guarded. "Yeah?"

"What does the X stand for?"

On the other line, the silence was deadening.

"Rich?" I said, "Still there?"

Silence. Then, "Nothing. It doesn't stand for anything."

"Like Harry S Truman?"

"Huh? Look, the story's this. My middle name is Stephens. That's my mother's maiden name."

"Uh-huh. Why do you use X—"

"Because my mother's dead. Stephens is no more."

And on that cheery note, he hung up.

Immediately, I called up Jessica and told her what Rich had said.

Her response was the same as Rich's. Silence. Finally, she said, "Oh my God."

"Do you think he's just trying to be intimidating or—"

"Charlie, he sounds psychotic."

"I have to live with this guy!"

"You can switch rooms," she said, "I mean, you can request a room change—"

"Yeah," I cut her off, "assuming I live long enough."

The night before I was to move into Montgomery, I had several dreams. They all dealt with Richard X Gulliver (who looked a bit like Eric Clapton back when he was the scary member of Cream) standing the middle of an empty room. "I've X'ed myself out of your world!" he screamed. Only after I woke up did I realize he was quoting Charles Manson.

And I, apparently, was to be Sharon Tate.

Montgomery Hall was filled with a motley collection of aspirers: aspiring musicians, aspiring writers, aspiring artists, and aspiring actors (like me). Of course, we were all going to grow up to become the type of people who bought designer jogging suits and drank waters from natural springs with names like Dominatrix. We all knew this but sometimes, you've got to play pretend.

Montgomery was among the oldest – if not the oldest – buildings on campus and it looked every hour of its age. From the outside, it was a mass of crumbling and cracked bricks. On the inside, the walls were stained with almost random splotches of sickly, brown spots. The building wasn't air-conditioned and a stagnant odor (decades of sweat, beer, tobacco, and pot) lingered in every hallway and crevice, as if to remind us of how many people had lived there before just to be forgotten once they left. My Dad, like all parents of Monties (that's what we called ourselves), hated it. That brought a certain sense of *fuck you* satisfaction.

When we arrived at my room, Rich was no where to be seen. However, on one of the two cots that passed for beds, there sat a green chest secured with a heavy, black lock.

"I guess that must be Rich's," I said. I hadn't told my Dad about my previous conversation with my new roommate. He said something about going to get the rest of my stuff but I barely heard him. I was too busy staring at that chest, wondering if perhaps it contained a real chest. (A sick pun? Rich hadn't sounded clever enough.)

Suddenly, a hoarse voice came from the hallway. "Oh, I see Charlie must be here!"

And Richard X Gulliver entered the room. To my surprise, he was a short, almost sickly figure. His voice didn't seem to go with his size. His hair was a curly, almost kinky blonde. His features were almost blandly homely; absolutely nothing about him stood out from any of the other Monties. Even his earring and the snake tattooed on his right arm seemed almost quaint.

He reached out and shook my hand. His grip was firm but he seemed too quick to retract his hand, as if he wanted to make sure he still had it.

"Rich?" I said.

"Yep, that's my name," he said. He was dressed in black – black boots, black jeans, black sleeveless shirt. "Don't wear it out." He laughed that forced laugh.

As my Dad dutifully brought up my stuff, I talked to Rich. Rich was certainly talkative but after a few minutes, his verbosity seemed to be more of a nervous tic than anything else. He told me he was a German major and he repeated that this was his third semester to be an incoming freshman. "I was having personal and financial problems," he helpfully explained. He was paying his way through college because of his stepmother (or "stepbitch" as he called her whenever my Dad wasn't around). He had an early afternoon job so he, therefore, had no choice but to sign up for early morning classes. "Early to bed, early to rise."

"Are you a light sleeper?" I asked, thinking of Jessica.

"The lightest," he replied.

By this point, my Dad had brought up my final box of possessions. For some reason, Rich chose this point to ask, "By the way, are you very religious?"

I could sense my Dad perking up behind me. He was very religious and so was I whenever he was around.

"Why?" I innocently replied.

"Well, I'm kinda the unofficial leader of the Montgomery Hall heathens, so—" His voice trailed off and he shrugged. "Well, I gotta go get the rest of my stuff."

He left. I turned to my Dad, tried to smile, and shrugged.

Rich didn't return until 9:30 that night (long after my Dad had returned home, probably a little relieved to have me out of the house). I had already visited Jessica over at Sapwood (and quickly left before either she or her mother could rope me into helping them unpack Jessica's mountain of material possessions).

When Rich returned, he brought with him more three more trunks. "This is all my stuff from my apartment," he explained, "I had to get it out of there before the landlord locked me out. I didn't pay rent this month."

The phone rang. Rich grabbed it and said, "Hello, Montgomery Hall Sweatshop. Huh? Oh yeah, he's here. Charlie, it's for you. Some girl."

I took the phone. "Jessica?"

"Was that Rich?" she asked.

"Yeah."

"He didn't sound like Eric Clapton. Or Charles Manson."

I glanced over at Rich and then whispered, "Nobody'll ever mistake him for God. You finished unpacking, yet?"

"Not even close. Can I call you later?"

"I'll be waiting, darlin'."

I hung up and was immediately faced with a laughing Rich. "Darlin'?" he chortled, "Hey, can I call you sweet-ums?"

"No."

Jessica called again sometime past midnight. Rich had gone to bed at 10:30 and as I answered the phone, Rich sat straight up in bed and stared at the ceiling.

I spoke to her in a low whisper, trying to ignore Rich's rigid pose and constant sighs. I talked to Jessica about the campus and about unpacking and we made naughty innuendoes as I withheld from using any pet names so as not to offend this new intruder in my life. We discussed the stupidity of Sapwood Hall's visitation policy (no male visitors past 1:00). "If you were here right now, what would you do to me?" she asked and I smiled my first real smile of the day. If nothing else, my relationship with Jessica offered me a lot of phone sex without having to worry about getting a heavy bill at the end of the month.

"Well," I started, "what do you want me—"

A loud groan belched through the room. It came from Rich as he fell down onto the bed and covered his head with a pillow.

"Jessica," I said, sweetly, "my roommate's getting pissed off."

"Oh – apologize to him for me."

"Sure, whatever," We hung up and I said to Rich, "Sorry about that."

"Yeah, whatever," Rich repeated my words, "Look, I think its fine and dandy that you two are so in love but I don't plan to spend any nights in the lobby just because you two kids are in here."

Kids? Of course, Rich was all of twenty-two.

"Are you going to be able to get back to sleep?" I asked.

"Yeah, if I meditate for a while."

And, legs crossed underneath him, he did just that.

I saw blessedly little of Richard X Gulliver over the next week, which was devoted to visiting bored academic advisors and signing up for classes that I knew I'd probably end up dropping after the first two weeks. I explored the campus with Jessica and I explored Jessica on the campus. When I walked by Rich on campus, we might occasionally nod but otherwise, we might as well have been total strangers. I quickly became used to the fact that when I would return from Sapwood (usually around 1:15 in the morning), Rich would sit straight up in bed and glare as I entered the room.

Occasionally, I would see him sitting in the Montgomery Hall Lobby, talking to the other Monties. He seemed to have quite a few friends as a result of his previous stabs at completing his freshman year. I have to admit that I was a little envious of him. I was still too shy to talk to anyone but Jessica.

One Thursday afternoon, I came to my room and discovered a sign had been posted on the door. Spread across a sheet of white paper, it was a declaration written in colored pencil. The handwriting was very small and almost excessively neat. I read it and then reread it.

Its Impossible To Start A Fire
If You Have No Desire To Burn

I stared at it. Rich, apparently, had a keen talent for the obvious. I unlocked the door and stepped into the room.

"You read my sign?" Rich asked. He was sitting, shirtless, on his bed.

"Oh," I feigned innocence, "you did that?"

"Yeah. What did you think?"

"Very profound, Rich."

"I try to put one up a week," Rich explained, "I have my opinions and I like to express them. No matter who it offends."

I couldn't believe I was nodding. "Yeah?"

"Yeah, I always get a few of the bible thumpers upset. They'll probably come knocking on the door in the middle of the night to keep me awake. Sorry about that. Of course, you're never here in the middle of the night anyway."

"There's bible thumpers in Montgomery, Rich?"

"A few. There's one right across the hall. Saw him walking around with holy book under his arm a couple of weeks ago. He seems sincere but I can't buy into that crap. Not after what happened to my mother."

"Oh."

"She died of cancer when I was eight—"

"I know, Rich."

"I told you?"

"Yeah, you told me. Three times."

"Oh."

The bible thumpers that Rich predicted never materialized but I made sure to keep my eyes open.

Jessica finally got to meet Rich the next night. She had come by the room several times over the previous week, usually just missing my roommate. On Monday, while he was meeting with his academic advisor, we had looked through his CD collection, finding it a bizarre combination of pre-Bon Scott AC/DC and men in kilts playing bagpipes. We had also checked out his meager book collection, which seemed to consist of books on World

War II and scholarly, scientific debunkings of the Bible. I told her of my fear that Rich might have been some Neo-Nazi atheist.

But anyway—

Jessica came up to the room while Rich was drowning himself in cheap cologne. He and some friends were planning to go down to Carver Street, BPU's center of drugs and fun. Rich barely looked at her when she entered, acknowledging her only enough to say, "So, you're the famous Jessica."

After Rich left, Jessica said, "He doesn't seem so bad."

"Did you see the sign on the door?" I asked.

"Yeah, I saw it. He's confused. A lot of people are."

I could have (perhaps should have) disagreed with her but, honestly, I had other things on my mind. I locked the door and, whispering all the pet names I was forbidden to repeat in Rich's presence, I kissed her.

About ten minutes later, we heard someone trying to open the door. This was followed by a loud banging which was followed by, "Hey, Charlie!"

Cursing, we fell out of the bed and pulled our clothes back on. Wearing my shirt inside out and running my hand through my unruly hair, I yelled, "Yeah, I'm coming!"

I glanced back at Jessica tucking her blouse back in. She nodded and I opened the door. Rich walked in and said, "Can you believe I forgot my key?"

I tried to be pleasant – God knows I did – as I replied, "No, I can't."

"Yeah," Then he added, "I don't think I'm going out, anyway."

"Why not?"

I could feel the look – a warning glance Jessica gave me when I was in danger of becoming a jerk – burning into the back of my neck.

"I can't get into that Carver Street lifestyle," Rich explained, gravely, "Can I tell you two something? Won't make you uncomfortable?"

"No, go ahead," Jessica said. I turned around and shot her a dirty look for encouraging him. She gave me a look back. Rich didn't seem to notice.

"Well," he started, "I've never had sex. I've never done any drugs, never smoked a cigarette, and I've been drunk once. And I'm comfortable with that. I'm not at all envious of those people down on Carver."

"That's nice, Rich," I muttered under my breath.

"That's very admirable, Rich," Jessica added.

Slowly, I sat down on the edge of my bed, helplessly watching as my night of passion disintegrated into some sort of morality parable. And I listened as this nonsmoking, bagpipe listening, atheistic, Neo-Nazi proceeded to have a nice, long (very nice, very long) conversation with my girlfriend. It wasn't that Jessica was flirting or that Rich was any more personable. His conversational skills still consisted of incomplete thoughts on randomly selected subjects. No, what annoyed me was that Jessica was actually smiling and coming up with plausible responses whereas I could rarely come up with anything other then "yeah" or a sarcastic comment; a wasted sarcastic comment as Rich had no real concept of irony, sarcasm, or anything else constituting humor. Actually, what truly upset me was that Jessica was talking to Rich and not declaring her undying love for Charlie. I sat there in silence as Rich said his main ambition was to be a househusband and raise his children. I listened as Jessica explained why she could never get a tattoo. "Well, I think a tattoo explains who you are," Rich was good enough to explain. And, as always, Rich bored us with his dead mother. Jessica nodded sympathetically as Rich detailed in long and painful detail how she died of lymph cancer. "So, yeah," Rich said, "I definitely support euthanasia."

"Oh yeah," Jessica nodded, "me too."

That was enough for me. I looked down at my watch and announced, the anger in my voice shocking even me, "Jessica, *darlin'*, I think its time to go."

Symbolically, or perhaps just unimaginatively, the night air was freezing as I escorted Jessica back to Sapwood Hall. Actually, "escort" is the wrong word. More like *led*. She had to know I was upset as we left Montgomery but instead she said those three words again: "Rich doesn't seem so bad."

"Yeah," I replied, "you two had a nice little conversation."

"He seemed talkative."

"So did you."

As we walked, I found myself moving faster and faster, throwing my legs further in front of me as I tried to channel all of that aggressive anger and jealousy that had been building up inside of me. Soon Jessica was far behind me and started to shout just to have words reach me but I didn't care. All I knew was that I hadn't gotten what I wanted and it made me furious.

As we neared Sapwood, I suddenly became aware that I was walking alone. I stopped and turned around. Jessica was standing a few feet behind me. Still moving in an angry stride, I returned to her.

"What's wrong?" I asked.

"You know what's wrong, Charlie. I didn't come here to be your girlfriend. Do you understand what I mean?"

I stared at her. Literally, I could not think. "So – what are you saying? You're breaking up with me?"

"Oh God no, Charlie. You being here; it's a wonderful bonus," she paused before continuing, "Except when you act like this but I put up with it because I love you."

"You do?"

"In a way. But you have to understand; I'm going to talk to other people. I'm going to have other friends. You will too. You have to. But I can't have my life just revolve around you. At least, not now. Do you understand?"

I nodded. My mouth was dry and a lump was forming in my throat as I realized just how close I'd come to losing her. "Yeah," I croaked, "I understand."

"All right. I'll see you tomorrow."

With that, she walked on to Sapwood Hall. Without me.

I guess, at this point, I'm coming across like a real jerk as far as Jessica was concerned. Well, I was young. Who wasn't a jerk when they were young? Besides, Jessica was the only girl I knew who laughed at all my jokes. I didn't like the thought of losing that.

After she told me she loved me "in a way," I ran around the campus for a while. Literally, running from building to building in an attempt to burn off more frustrated energy before I had to deal with any more human interaction.

When I returned to Montgomery, Rich was sitting in the lobby talking to some fat slob who lived on our wing and spent most of his time obnoxiously whistling. Rich actually talked to me (though he didn't introduce me to his corpulent buddy). He was off from work tomorrow so I could stay up as late as I wanted. I was lucky, Rich assured me, to have such a charming girlfriend. How I wanted to kill him there in that lobby. However, for legal reasons, I resisted.

Instead, I went up to the room and called Jessica. When she answered, I said, "I'm sorry."

"Charlie?"

"I'm sorry, Jessica," I repeated, "I won't ever treat you like that again. I promise."

"Okay, sweetie—" Pet names! *SCREW YOU, RICH!* "I'll see you tomorrow."

We both hung up and I got into bed. I asked God to make me a better boyfriend – Religion! *SCREW YOU TWICE, RICH!* – and then fell asleep.

That weekend, Jessica and I returned home. In between re-galing my Dad with stories (true and false) of wild campus life, I discovered I had forgotten my key to the dorm room. I called Rich around 8:00 on Saturday night.

After nine rings, he picked up.

"Yeah?" His voice was draggy.

"Hey, Rich, this is your roommate."

"Yeah, I know your voice, Charlie."

"Listen, I left my key up there."

"Yeah, I saw it."

"Well, could you do me a favor and not lock up the room on Sunday night so I can still get in—"

Long pause. "Yeah, I guess so."

"Thanks, Rich."

"Yeah, listen, Charlie, I can't live like this, man."

"Well—" How does one respond to bullshit like this? – "it won't happen again."

"Yeah." *Click.*

I sighed. This was going to be a long semester.

Except that it wasn't. Actually, that first semester ended up going by very quickly. This was probably because I dropped (or skipped) most of my classes. I was left with a lot of free time to play with Jessica. Play we did. Within the first few weeks, we discovered a dreadfully pretentious coffeehouse called the End of the World. It stayed open twenty-four hours a day so we would hang out there and be arty until around four in the morning when I would walk her to Sapwood. We'd make out on the front steps, and then I'd make my way back to Montgomery where I would sit in the lobby and work up the courage to go to my room and risk waking up Rich. The thing of it was that I did know it was dreadfully insensitive of me to wake Rich up every single night. I understood it but I didn't particularly care. I was young and in love and the rest of the world could go to Hell.

At 4:30, I would try to sneak into the room as quietly as possible and at 4:31, Rich would sit straight up in his bed like a wind-up toy. I would tiptoe over to my bed while Rich groaned with every squeak of my shoes. I would undress and leave my clothes on the floor and I knew that Rich was silently cursing me for leaving my half of the room such a disorganized mess. Again, I knew all of this but I didn't care.

As promised, each week brought a new bit of wisdom from the fertile mind of Richard X Gulliver. Most of it was mundane (*Given the Choice Between Truth and Faith, I'll Take Truth*) and some of it was incoherent (*If God's Chairman of the Board, Then Satan's a Monkey's Uncle*).

Eventually, I resorted to decorating my side of the door. Every week, Jessica and I would go down to the local grocery store and pick up a copy of the *Weekly World News*. Searching the paper, we'd find and cut out a picture that caught our fancy and tape it on the door beside Rich's latest proclamation. Hence, on any given day, a door reader might come across "*Man is the Ultimate God*," with "*Aliens Visit Alan Alda For Gender Equality Conference*" posted right beside.

Rich, for all his faults, wasn't stupid and he quickly figured out what we were doing. He posted a sign at the top of the door reading, "*In Loving Memory, This Door And All Of Its Contents Are Dedicated To The Memory Of Victoria Stephens Gulliver.*" After that, Jessica and I stopped buying the *Weekly World News*.

I'm not exactly sure when this happened. However, since it occurred when I was still enrolled in my afternoon psychology class, it must have been early in the semester. I was returning to Montgomery when I ran into Rich, walking out the front doors. "Jessica's up in the room," he said. For some reason, I noticed that his eyes were even more blank than usual.

"Thanks, Rich," I said, "you okay?"

"Have to go see my Stepbitch for the weekend."

"Oh."

Long pause.

Rich said, "It sucks," and then walked on. I entered Montgomery and ran upstairs to my room, suddenly concerned that Rich had murdered my girlfriend. Luckily, I found her alive, sitting at my computer and looking through my private files.

After fooling around for a bit (It had become a routine and at that time, I had no idea that this could actually be a bad thing), Jessica told me, "Rich said I was beautiful."

"What?" She was lying on top of me as she said this, "When?"

"When I came by. He was working on one of his signs and I apologized for interrupting and he said, 'That's okay. Its not everyday a beautiful girl knocks on my door.'"

Jessica was flattered and I guess I should have been impressed that other people found my girlfriend as attractive as I did. Instead, it angered me; this nut who barely said six words a day to me, hitting on my woman.

If Rich and I ever did any bonding, it had to be when we both started dropping our classes. We would sit at our respective desk, filling out drop forms and bitching about asshole professors. One day, he entered the room, walked over to my desk, and dropped an extra slip on it. "Here's an extra just in case," he explained. Actually, what he said was far wittier but I've forgotten it over time. Unfortunate when you consider that was the only interesting thing Rich said that semester.

Unfortunately, the more classes we dropped, the more free time we had. I would spend most of my time auditing Jessica's art history classes in an effort to have more to talk to her about. After all, our relationship wasn't just about sex alone. Or at least that was what I kept telling myself.

Rich spent his extra hours in the room, coming up with new signs and often sitting on his bed in a meditative position or staring blankly up at the ceiling. Often, I would come walking down the hallway, towards our room, and I would hear AC/DC blasting. Rich would play his CDs on my player with the volume turned up as high as it would go. As he listened to the music (usually *Highway to Hell*), he would pace as if in a trance, seemingly oblivious to anyone entering the room. In my mind, his use of my CD player justified the fact that I would sometimes steal his shampoo or any quarters he might occasionally leave sitting out on his desk. *Quid pro quo.*

(Whatever that might mean.)

And this is how things progressed until, halfway through the semester, Richard X Gulliver found God.

Brandon Ostrowlski lived across the hall from us. He was the "bible thumper" that Rich had railed against at the beginning of the semester. A senior, he was a tall guy with curly brown hair and a quick, friendly smile that often seemed to clean to be sincere. Yet sincere it was. He was a music education major and his door was decorated with pictures of Dizzy Gillepse. I think the fact that he was a walking jazz encyclopedia helped the Monties accept him as one of their own despite the fact that he regularly led a bible study group in the lobby.

Jessica and I had first met Brandon about three weeks into the semester. He had shook our hands and invited us to some meeting of the Christian Monties or something of that sort. The invitation had been nice and direct. No attempts were made to soften us up, make us feel guilty, or intimidate us with visions of Hell. We agreed to go though in the end, we ended up spending the night fooling around in her room instead. However, Brandon never gave either of us a hard time about it and he still greeted me everyday with that some unbelievable smile. As the semester progressed, I found myself wishing that Brandon had been my roommate instead. Actually, I still do.

I don't know when or even why Rich and Brandon became friends. Brandon, of course, knew of Rich's enthusiastic disbelief. Whenever he saw Rich standing in the hallway, taping up one of his sayings, Brandon would say, "Hey, Rich." After a month and a half, Rich actually returned the greeting. Soon, I would regularly discover the two of them standing out in the hallway talking.

I knew something was changing when a week began and no new saying was posted on the door. As I stood before my door and marveled at the blankness before me, Brandon stepped out into the hall.

"Hey, Charlie," he said, "nice door?"

"There's nothing to read," I replied, "There's no new weekly wisdom to digest."

"Yeah, I convinced him to hold off until bible study tonight."

"Rich is going to bible study?"

"I talked him into it."

I laughed. "How?"

Brandon shrugged. "I said, 'Rich, you wanna come to bible study tonight?' and he said, 'Sure.' Y'see, Rich has always believed. You can't hate a God you don't believe in."

Brandon then invited me to bible study as well. I can't remember what excuse I came up with but I'm sure it was a good one.

That night, while Rich was gone, I went through his desk in a search for any loose change. I found the note, neatly folded into four squares, sitting in the back of the bottom drawer. I fished it out and unfolded it.

It was signed *Brandon* and began *Rich, I know you're angry at God right now.* I stopped, suddenly aware that I shouldn't have been reading this. Quickly, I refolded it and placed it back in the drawer.

Rich came to the room that night at 10:30, carrying a heavy bible which he proceeded to read in bed for the next hour or so. Though he said nothing to me, I could tell he was different. He seemed calmer, almost at peace.

Nothing went up on the door that week or the weeks after.

At the same time as Rich's conversion, Jessica and I started to fight. We fought over the number of classes I dropped or skipped. We fought over politics, over sex, over her friends, over everything. But the main reason we were fighting was because Jessica wanted to move on. We'd been dating for over a year and it was becoming increasingly obvious that I would never magically become the man she wanted to spend the rest of her life with. At the time, I knew this and would have done anything to become that man, short of actually changing.

That night, we fought because I didn't properly comb my hair. I kid you not. I had met her at the University Library to "help" her study. I splashed on some cologne and when I walked up to her table, I smiled and winked.

She coolly looked me over, sniffed, and said, "If you're going to put on cologne and wink at me, you could at least comb your hair."

I was quiet for a few minutes. Never had somebody who claimed to care about me said something so frigidly cruel. Finally, I managed to croak out, "Bitch."

"I don't have time to be insulted by you," she replied, returning her attention to the textbooks spread out in front of her.

I ran out of the library and back to my room. I slammed the door as I entered. Rich was lying in bed in his new pose, reading his bible.

"Hey, Charlie," he said. Religion had made him much more talkative.

I didn't reply. I fell down on my bed and closed my eyes, wishing I was back home where I knew everybody and my lover didn't seem intent on destroying me.

"You okay?" Rich asked.

I opened my eyes and looked at him. He was standing by the door, about to leave for bible study.

"Jessica and I had a fight," I said.

He laughed. "Another one?"

"Another one?"

Rich laughed again. "You crazy kids—" He actually said this! "—y'know, Charlie, you better be careful or she might end up leaving you."

I sat up. "What did you say?"

"I'm going to be late."

He turned his back to me. Jumping to my feet, I grabbed his shoulder and spun him around. "Whaa—?" he gasped as I slammed him up against the wall. His eyes were wide and his mouth hung dumbly open. He was scared. I had taken him by surprise. Shit, I'd taken myself by surprise.

"What the FUCK did you just say!?" I was screaming in his face.

"Let go of me, dammit!"

Rich managed to squirm free from my grasp and coiled back his fist. I prepared myself for impact.

And then nothing happened.

Rich lowered his fist and said, "I'm turning the other cheek, Charlie."

He left for bible study.

Jessica called me that night and apologized. I apologized to her and we both cried over the phone and declared our eternal love for each other, mostly because that was what we were supposed to do. I really should have apologized to Rich as well but I didn't. Why? Well, for starters, I wasn't sleeping with Rich.

Rich and I talked even less after that incident. He spent most of his time in Brandon's room. He still talked to his old Monty friends in the lobby but when he wasn't around, I'd hear them mention his name and rudely laugh. Once, I caught them giving his back the finger as he was walking away.

He stopped listening to AC/DC. He'd tracked down a used copy of the *Jesus Christ Superstar* soundtrack and now he obsessively played it, full volume on my CD player. He still entered the same trance when listening to his music. Only the soundtrack to his catatonia was now *I Don't Know How To Love Him* instead of *Highway to Hell*.

And every night, he would lie in his bed and read his bible. Before going to sleep, he'd loudly pray for the souls of everyone he knew on campus, naming each one personally. He included Jessica in that list. I took me about a week to notice that the only person he didn't mention was me.

As the semester entered its final month, something changed
at Montgomery Hall. The Monties, usually mellow to excess,
were collectively realizing that their chances to pass their classes
and maintain good GPAs were becoming increasingly slim. Soon,
the lobby was full of science study groups and math tutors. The
halls, once filled with the sounds of music, arguments, and or-
gasms, were now eerily silent. Everyone was too busy trying to
save their ass to sample their CD collections.

Everyone except for Rich. He still blasted Andrew Lloyd
Webber every afternoon and the only book he opened was his
bible. Even Brandon eventually asked him if he was studying.

"I'm praying," Rich replied.

"Next semester," Jessica said to me, "try to get a private room."

I had come from my English class to get some dinner. Jessica
was waiting for me in the lobby. She looked exhausted.

"Why?" I asked, "What did Rich do?"

Jessica told me her story. She'd come by the room looking
for me and found Rich standing outside, sweating and breathing
heavily. She asked him what was wrong.

"I couldn't stay in that room anymore," he told her, "Charlie
won't clean his side of the room—" and then he proceeded to list
every single thing I'd done wrong over the semester: staying up
late, losing my key, dropping my clothes everywhere, using his
shampoo, etc., etc.

"The whole time," she said, "I was wondering what he ex-
pected me to do about it."

I nodded, my rage boiling up inside me. Not once had Rich
mentioned these concerns to me; or at least not recently. No, he
had dumped all of this on my girlfriend. At a time when Jessica
and I were struggling to find a reason – any reason – to stay
together, Rich had done this.

I wanted to kill him.

I ate dinner in silence. After escorting Jessica back to Sapwood, I stalked my way to Montgomery. I went up to my room and found Rich lying in bed, reading his bible.

He barely glanced at me as I walked over to his bed.

"Close the bible, Rich," I said.

"What?"

"Close the fucking bible."

"Why?"

"Because I don't want to feel sacrilegious when I kill you. Close the bible."

Rich closed the bible. Laying it across his chest, he asked, "What's up?"

"If you've got any problem with me," I was spitting the words out, "then come to me. Leave Jessica out of this."

Suddenly, Rich was on his feet. The bible fell to the floor with a thud. "I had to tell someone—"

"Jessica doesn't need to deal with your crap right now, Rich! You want this fucking room clean!? Then clean it yourself!" I was screaming at him, "But leave my girlfriend – *my* girlfriend, Rich, not yours, mine! – out of it!"

"I just needed to talk—"

"Why don't you tell your God, Rich!?"

I think I heard the crack of his fist smashing into my face before I felt it or was even aware of what was happening. I stumbled back and felt myself falling onto my bed.

Rich was at my side. "Oh God," he said, his voice almost childlike, "Oh God, I'm sorry."

He ran out of the room. I'd like to think that he was ashamed, that his apologies were meant for me. Maybe they were. Or maybe, he meant exactly what he said. *God, I'm sorry.*

Now, you may be wondering why I stayed in the room. Why didn't I go find a hotel room for the remaining month or move down to the lobby or live in Jessica's closet? God knows I thought about it but for some reason, I stayed in the room. Maybe it was morbid curiosity.

I had a black eye for about a week. Jessica asked about it and, like a battered wife, I lied and said I'd run into a door. Rich, of course, apologized to me and I apologized to him. I cleaned my end of the room and again, swore to avoid him. After all, there were only four weeks left.

Two days later, as I was walking down to my room, I saw a fellow Monty standing in front of the door, staring at something and stroking his beard. As I reached him, I saw what he was looking at. A piece of paper had been posted, dead center, on the door.

The guy barely looked at me as I read it. The handwriting was Rich's.

Dear God:
I am not worthy to be your servant.
My sins against you and others
Are legion and I cannot ask you to
Forgive me and to love me
While so many others are in pain.
So many others deserve and need you
More and I do not understand how
You could love someone like me.
God, there are times when I wish
You would just smite me from the Earth
And punish me for my trespass.
I do not deserve to be your child.
Amen.

"Is this your room?" the guy asked.

"Uh, yeah," I said, "but I didn't write that. I guess my room-mate did."

"Man, that's some weird shit."

As we spoke, others were walking down the hall. They all stopped to read Rich's words and most smiled smugly and some displayed their wit by doing overly familiar impersonations of TV evangelists. That fat guy who was always whistling read the prayer and said, "Rich has really gone off the deep end."

I shrugged. What could I say? At least he didn't think I'd written it.

"Y'know," the whistler continued, "maybe you should put a set of razor blades by his bed tonight." Rich's friend started whistling and continued on his way.

I ducked into the room, locking the door behind me. Rich wasn't in the room. That relieved me. I'd expected to either find him dead or waiting to smite me from the Earth. I thought about calling Jessica and asking her what to do but I decided against it. She didn't need to be dragged any further into this.

I studied for a couple of hours, believe it or not. Rich was nowhere to be seen. His bible was sitting on his bed, next to his *Jesus Christ Superstar* CD. Finally, somebody knocked on the door.

Cautiously, I went to the door and asked, "Who is it!?"

"Brandon!" came the response, "Is Rich here? I need to talk to him."

I opened the door and answered, "No, I don't know where he is."

Brandon nodded and then asked, "You read the note?"

"Yeah, I read it."

"Little freaky, huh?" Brandon stepped into the room as he spoke, "I'm going to have to talk to him. The thing with people like Rich is that they're so desperate to have something to believe in that when they find it, they go to extremes. Now, I've got to set him right without losing him."

I nodded, though the words meant little to me. I didn't care why Rich was Rich. I just wanted something done about him.

"Hey guys," Rich suddenly said. He was standing in the doorway. "How's it going, Brandon?"

"Rich," Brandon said, "we need to talk."

Glancing down at my watch, I lied, "I've got to go meet Jessica down at the library." I ducked out of the room.

Alone, I sat down in the lobby for about an hour. Finally, I saw Brandon heading for the cafeteria and went back upstairs to my room.

When I stepped into the hallway, the first thing I heard was AC/DC blasting at full volume. The Monty who had first pointed out the prayer to me was now standing in front of my newly bare door.

He shouted to me over the music, "Your roommate came outside and ripped off the note!"

"Oh yeah?" I replied.

"Yeah, he was pissed!"

I stepped into the room. Rich was in his pacing trance. In our trashcan sat both his bible and *Jesus Christ Superstar.*

Rich and I literally didn't say one word to each other for the rest of the semester. The month passed quickly and I spent most of my time at Jessica's, studying for what few finals I had. Rich, as far as I know, spent his time listening to *Highway to Hell.*

The Wednesday of the final week should have been a good day for me. My English final had been a breeze, Jessica was nearly finished with her finals, and Rich was gone. He'd taken all his finals, moved his stuff back to his old apartment, and thoroughly cleaned his half of the room. That afternoon, before leaving for English, I'd silently cheered as I watched Rich turn his room key into the front desk.

I met Jessica for dinner in the Montgomery Hall cafeteria. As we ate, she sat silently and I knew she was going to hurt me before the meal was over.

"Charlie," she finally said, "what are you going to do when this is all over?"

I shrugged and tried to avoid what I knew was coming. "Go home?"

Jessica nodded. "Go ahead and joke. You know what I mean."

"Dammit. Okay, Jessica, tell me. What am I going to do?"

"I don't know," She sighed with a melodramatic flourish, making sure I understood how difficult this was for her. Jessica was a girl of many talents, one of the most prominent being the ability to find victimhood in every situation. "But you realize it has to end, don't you? I mean, I have to find – I'm sorry, Charlie, I just can't see myself spending the rest of my life with you."

I sat there, dumbfounded. Finally, I was able to say, "Why not?"

"Charlie, you can't even handle a roommate for one semester!"

She finished eating quickly and then left, saying she had to study. I went up to my room, feeling neither sad, angry, nor free. I felt nothing. The break-ups, the angst, all the bullshit that our relationship had become could no longer produce any emotion inside of me. It was all too predictable.

The room seemed bare without Rich's stuff. My mess – discarded clothes, dropped books, crumpled papers – still sat over in my corner but it now seemed dwarfed by the rest of the room. As I looked across the expanse, I realized that for the first time since leaving home, I was actually alone. It was a solitude that I could hear blowing across the room like a desert wind.

I went over to Rich's former desk to see if he'd left behind any spare change. Sitting on the desktop was a note written in Rich's precise handwriting. He listed what he had cleaned for the final checkout (sink, floorboard) and what I had left to do (everything else). At the bottom of the note, Rich had added:

P.S. Charlie, it really sucked living with you this semester. – Rich.

I went back home the next day. A week later, grades came. My GPA was 2.5. Jessica's was a 4.0.

Brandon graduated that semester. He came back to Montgomery Hall a year later to visit some old friends. I didn't talk to him but I later heard he was an elementary school music teacher in Oklahoma.

Jessica officially dumped me over the Christmas Break. I didn't quite believe it until the spring semester started and she started dating some blonde frat boy. I'd see them walking across campus together and I'd have to admit they made a cute couple in a bland, pop music sort of way. Sometimes I'd smile and wave and sometimes, Jessica would wave back. Eventually, she'd dump that frat boy and she'd come back to me. And again, she dumped me before coming back to me. It was an increasingly dull cycle we played out over the years even as we forgot what had made us so special to begin with. We were just a pair of habits.

You probably expect me to report that Rich ended up blowing his brains out in the Montgomery Lobby while all the Monties stared on in postmodern apathy. Well, that hasn't happened. At least not yet. After the end of that first semester, I had only two encounters with Rich.

At the beginning of the next semester, I came across a letter in the university newspaper. It loudly complained that the library placed books on witchcraft in the occult section instead of the religion section where they belonged. It was signed Richard X Gulliver.

Two months later, I was standing in front of the Student Union watching some frat ceremony for world peace or something of that sort. Imagine a large group of blonde football players lighting unity candles. I was watching Jessica's new boyfriend, imagining his violent death, when I heard a hoarse voice behind me.

"That's a little too Greek for me."

I turned around. Rich Gulliver smiled at me and nodded. I nodded back.

And with that, Rich went on his way.

LEST WE FORGET . . .

Prof. Kenneth Slate explains the concept of the Yin and the Yang to his Monday night Introduction to Philosophy Class.

"The Yin," Slate says, "is considered to be positive, white, aggressive, dry, and male. The Yang is negative, black, passive, wet, female."

From the back of the class, sophomore Taylor Smith says, "Well, I don't see what's so negative about a passive, wet female."

Slate frowns even as a few of the males in the class chuckle and shake their head in disbelief that Taylor actually said aloud what they were thinking. The females in the class sigh in moral outrage. Proudly, Taylor sits back. Little aware is he that, in his remaining fifty-seven years of life, this is the wittiest thing he will ever say.

CLOUD COVERS

Last weekend as I was stumbling back
To my home after a day and an evening
Of relaxation and mind alteration
I stared up at the blue sky
And I realized that the clouds
Were following me
I stood still
And the clouds hung in place
In the sky without a sign of life
I stepped back two feet
And the clouds moved with me
I jumped forward my head to the sky
And the clouds rushed to keep up
And I ran in a zigzag across the land
And the clouds made themselves dizzy
And I stared up there
Pondering my powers
And my newly discovered
But age-old role
As God, master of all
And I closed my eyes
To hear the content of the faithful's prayers
I listened to the bereaved begging
Charlie, please bring my loved ones back
And somewhere in New Jersey
A college student on academic probation
Charlie, please get me an A in Pre-Cal
And deep in France a virgin asks

Charlie, please help me get laid tonight
And multitudes across the world
Charlie, please make the violence stop
And the voices blended into one migraine
So I reopened my eyes
Stared at the sky
And decided to play with the clouds
Some more

FEBRUARY 17TH, 1993

Walking back to my apartment, I ran into Abdil, a friend from last semester's Milton Seminar, getting high behind Montgomery Hall. "Y'know," Abdil said, "most people don't like you. But I like you. I tell them, yes, Charlie Wax is an evil, disgusting person but at least he's honest about it." I smiled and replied, "Or else I'm a nice guy who's a really good liar."

MOWING THE LAWN

BLLPPP!

Sounds are drifting in through my window.

BLLPPP!

It's six in the morning.

BLLPPP!

It's a *lawnmower*. Who mows their lawn at six in the morning?

BLLPPP!

My neighbor does. I stumble out of bed and head for the window. Fat, middle-aged, bald Ted "What a Great Day To Buy Insurance" Whithers is standing in his yard, cussing out his lawnmower. He gives the ripcord another rough yank.

BLLPPP! DROOOOOOOONE!!

The mower shakes to life and Ted, looking content with his accomplishment, starts to push the cutting machine across his pristinely green lawn. Aw Hell, its Saturday, isn't it? Everyone in Glory Hole mows his lawn on Saturday. It's some sort of un-written law. Shit.

It's ten in the A.M. and I'm sitting in my living room, smoking a Marlboro Red. I hate smoking inside. Smoke gets in the air conditioning vents and soon the whole house is flooded with haze. But I can't stand the idea of being outside on Saturday. All those cursed husbands and son-in-laws marching in perfect unison as they push their mowers across their yards; the sight sickens me. They always make me think of the slaves on the Roman galley in *Ben-Hur*. At least the slaves had Charlton Heston on their side.

DING-DONG!

Somebody's at the front door. I sink down into the couch and hope they'll go away.

DING-DING-DING-DING-DING-DONG!

Damn, damn, damn! I walk to the front door and unlock the first lock, the second lock, and the third lock. Standing on the front porch, Chet Rainey's little brother, Herbie, looks up at me and grins like a cherubic angel. I think he's ten.

"Hiya, Mr. Wax," he says.

Mr. Wax!? When did I get old? Little bastard must want something.

"I'm only twenty, Herbie," I tell him, "Don't call me mister."

A steady **DROOONE!** pollutes the air. Across the street, James "Just Like The Singer" Brown stands out in his yard, shirtless (thanks a lot, James!) and trying to start his lawnmower.

"Mr. Wax," Herbie starts, "my youth group is selling cookies for the Daughters of Glory Hole—"

"Wait a minute, Herbie. Does this mean you and your little friends are going to be bugging me so you can win a trip to Philadelphia or something—"

"No, we're going to Chicago!" Herbie's grin gets even wider. His chubby face looks like it might split down the middle if he gets any more wholesome.

"Does that mean all of you little bastards are going to be coming by here, trying to make me buy your cookies?"

"Not if you buy from me!" For a ten year-old, Herbie's pretty smooth.

"Do the cookies still taste like cardboard, Herbie? I bought a dozen boxes from you last year. Eventually, I had to throw the damn things out. They were starting to organize."

"Everyone else on the block is buying them!" Herbie suddenly whines. I glare down at him and he tries to grin again. Sorry, Herbie. Spell's been broken.

"Sorry, Herbie."

"But, Mr. Wax, if we don't win—"
I close the door in his face and finish off my cigarette.

BANG! BANG! BANG!
I turn off the TV right in the middle of a classic episode of *Jackson and Mr. P*; the one where Jackson becomes a Black Panther and accuses his adoptive father of being just another guilty, white liberal from Park Avenue. I go to the living room window to see who's knocking on my door. My God, the blonde Adonis himself is standing out on my front porch and he's even banging on my door! Still wearing his old High School football jacket, Chet Rainey still looks like the guy who used to spend Study Hall shooting spit wads at me. I go to the entrance, unlock the first lock, the second lock, and the third. I open the door.

"Hey, guy," Chet smiles, "what's up?"
I notice he's wearing a ragged t-shirt that reads *I SURVIVED COACH YABLONSKI'S VARSITY FOOTBALL TEAM*. Shit, when was the last time Chet talked to me? Two years ago at graduation, I think. His exact words, I believe, were "Get outta my way, asshole!"

Chet continues, "I haven't seen you around in a while, man."
"Yeah," I shrug, "been keeping to myself—"
"That's cool. You in school?"
"No." Tempting to tell him the truth about what I'm doing this semester while I should be in school. Taking a few months off, watching my Dad's house for him, trying to dry out after drinking away the last of my teen years, wondering why I keep waking up with a hangover if I'm sober, using too many fucking gerunds. But I don't go into it.
"Working?" he asks.
"No."
"That's cool," Chet keeps on smiling through all this. A Rainey family trademark, that smile is. "Well, anyway, I'm home for the weekend from SMU and—"
"You still playing football over there?"

"Uh, no," the smile disappears briefly before flashing back, "Not this semester, anyway. Look, Wax, my brother says you won't buy any of his cookies."

"I don't want any of his cookies."

The smile goes away and doesn't come back. I want to close the door. The air outside smells like freshly cut grass and the only sound I can hear is that constant **DROOONE!** of hardworking mowers.

"Look," Chet says, "my brother's been working really hard to win that trip to Chicago so why don't you just be a pal and buy his cookies, okay?"

"I bought them last year. They're awful."

"You don't have to eat them! Get some pets and feed them the damn cookies! Look, I don't mean to spazz out here but you've got my brother crying. So, why don't you just stop acting like a dick and buy his fucking cookies? Okay, buddy?"

I start to close the door but Chet jams his foot into the doorway. Over his shoulder, I see a rusted lawnmower. Sitting in my own overgrown lawn, it seems to glare at me with a righteous rage. *This grass is ankle-length! Weeds have entered the perimeter! How,* it shouts, *HOW COULD YOU LET THIS HAPPEN!?*

"Look, Wax," Chet's still talking, I realize. "Everyone else has bought a box, okay? Why don't you just be a good guy and—"

I slam my boot down on his foot. He pulls back and I slam the door. Lock one, lock two, lock three, safely hidden. I go back to the couch and catch the end of *Jackson and Mr. P.*

Those cookies taste like cardboard. I'm justified.

DING-DONG!

I wait until *Jackson and Mr. P* (they're showing a marathon, bless them) breaks for commercial before I unlock the door. Its Mrs. O'Connor, whose homosexual, middle-aged son comes up to Glory Hole every weekend to mow her lawn.

"Hello, Davey," she says. She thinks my name is David so she calls me Davey. Of course, my name is Charles so the proper affectionate nickname is Charlie but fuck it.

"Hey, Mrs. O'Connor," I reply.

"Davey, would you stop out onto the front porch with me for a few minutes?"

"Outside?"

"Yes, Davey, outside."

I step out onto the front porch. Mrs. O'Connor looks out over my yard.

"Y'know, Davey," she starts, "its not good just leave your lawnmower out there like that. It's already starting to rust."

"I was planning on taking it in," I lie.

"Your lawn could stand for a little mowing but that's your own business, I suppose."

I nod in agreement. Out on the porch, I can see the entire block. Suburban house after suburban house. Row after row after row of large, green lawns that almost glow. And on each lot of grass – marching in the same strict, orderly pattern – are the sweat-soaked slaves with lawnmowers.

"Davey," Mr. O'Connor continues, "I just got finished talking to little Herbie Rainey and he is just in tears! He says you won't buy any cookies from him."

Charlie, Davey, Herbie, I feel like I'm trapped in a fucking Andy Hardy movie.

"Those cookies taste like cardboard, Mrs. O'Connor."

"Yes, Davey, we all know that. That's not what this is about. Herbie is convinced that he's lost his youth group their chance of going to Chicago."

"I've never been to Chicago," I say as I light a cigarette.

"That's because you never sold cookies, Davey. It's your business if you want to smoke but you please spare my lungs the pleasure of your second-hand smoke?"

"Sorry," I say, flipping the cigarette into a nearby patch of fungus.

"Herbie also tells me that his older brother – you know Chet from school, don't you? – came over to speak with you and you got very abusive. The entire Rainey family is very displeased with you and quite frankly, so am I."

Somewhere, I can hear someone else trying to start up his lawnmower.

"Davey, are you listening to me?" Mrs. O'Connor asks.

"Yeah. Look, I don't have anything against the Raineys." Other than the fact that I hate them. "But I don't want any cookies."

"And for that, little Herbie Rainey has to feel like a failure. Is that what you're saying?"

I shrug. "I guess so."

Mrs. O'Connor sighs and rolls her eyes heavenward. "Davey, before your parents moved, they would buy cookies every year. Did you know that?"

"Then why doesn't Herbie go bug them?"

Mrs. O'Connor sighs again and shakes her blue head. "Okay, okay, I've done everything I can do. I just hope you'll give what I said a little extra thought."

"Sure thing."

Still shaking her head, Mrs. O'Connor leaves my porch, glares at my lawnmower, and then head back to her own house. Quickly, I duck inside, lock the door, and turn on the TV. I'm just in time to catch the end credits of *Jackson and Mr. P.*

Damn.

CRRRRRAAASSSSH!

I throw myself flat to the floor as the window shatters and shards of glass crash around me. Listening for a second attack, I lie there.

DROOOOONE!

The silence of my living room has been destroyed. All that can be heard are seemingly hundreds of lawn mowers circulating outside my house. All that can be smelled is freshly cut grass.

HONK! HONK!
HEY, FAGGOT! OUT HERE, FAGGOT!
In my window, there's a jagged hole.
DROOOOONE! BLLLP! BLLLP! BLLLP! HONK!
HONK! DROOOONE! FAGGOT! DROOOOONE! HEY,
WAX, YOU FUCKING FAGGOT! DROOOONE! OUT
HERE, FAGGOT! DROOOONE! HONK! DROOONE!
There's a large, heavy stone lying in my living room. Cautiously, I pick it up.
DROOOOONE! HONK! HONK! WAX!
There's a string tied around the rock and at the other end of the string, a box of cookies. Buttermilk wafers to be exact. *Compliments of the Daughters of Glory Hole.*
C'MON, YOU FAGGOT! OUT HERE!
I go to the window. There's a pickup truck standing outside my house. The motor is running and the exhaust fills the air, mixing with the scent of freshly mowed grass. In the front cab are two guys I vaguely recognize. Both are blonde, muscular, and wearing Glory Hole High School football jackets. Standing in the back of the truck, giving me the finger, is Chet Rainey.

"There's your fucking cookies!" Chet yells at me. He's swaying and I can see he's holding an empty beer bottle. "Now, go pay my fucking brother, you fucking faggot!"

The other two guys smirk and give me the finger as well. The pickup truck suddenly roars to life, disappearing down the street.

I leap to the front door and try to dramatically fling it open. No such luck. It's locked. Quickly, I unlock the door. Lock two. Lock one. Lock three. Throwing open the door, I run out in my front yard. The truck and Chet Rainey are gone. As the thick grass brushes against my knees, I turn back to my house and stare at the gaping hole in the window.
BLLLPPPP!
I swing around, looking for the source of the sound.
BLLLLPPPP!

Across the street, some fat bastard tries to start his lawnmower.
BLLLLLPPPP!!!!!
I stare at him. His large stomach sags over the wide waist-
band of his shorts and his pale skin jiggles each time he pulls the
ripcord.
BLLLLPPPPP!
"You mowed your lawn last week!" I yell at him.
DROOOONNNNEEE!
Carefully and precisely, he pushes his mower across his yard,
seemingly aware neither of me nor the box of cardboard cookies
that's just destroyed my sanctuary.
I swing around to face my own judgmental lawnmower.
Running up to it, I yank on its ripcord.
BLLLPPP!
The corroded machine shakes a little.
BLLLPPP!
The motor struggles to find some life and I give it one last try.
BLLLLPPPP! DROOOOONE!
I scan my yard. Pushing the gasping mower in front of me, I
run up to the upper right hand corner before taking a sharp turn
and heading down the other way. I take another sharp turn be-
fore starting to dance in a random, zigzag pattern across my lawn.
A wave of grassy debris flies past me as I start to spin around
in circles and the mower's steady **DROONNEEE!** is interrupted
by a sputtering cough coming from the spinning blades. Next
door, I see old Mrs. Healy standing out on her porch. She's put-
ting on her thick glasses and staring at me. I wave to her and
shout, "Beautiful day to mow the lawn!" but she can't hear me
over the mower.
Another turn and I can hear the sound of random twigs,
gravel, and ants being sliced out of existence beneath me. There's
Mrs. O'Connor, standing across the street with a puffy-faced
Herbie Rainey. They both give me stern looks of disapproval. I
shake my fist at them and shout, "Burn, baby, burn!" Why? Don't
know. Seems appropriate.

Finally, exhausted from randomly chopping up my yard, I bring the lawnmower to a stop and collapse onto my porch. I stare out at the ravaged plot of land that now surrounds my house.

Silence.

There's not one sound in the air.

Complete silence.

Strike that. There's a bird chirping. There's always a bird chirping, isn't there?

Not one lawnmower.

They're all standing out in the neat, beautiful lawns in front of their neat, beautiful houses and they're all staring at me as if I've been possessed by something truly unholy. Nobody says anything. They just stare as I wipe the sweat off my brow. I am the center of their world. I have taken them away from their lawns. Me.

Silence. Still air. A bird chirping. Blissful silence.

BLLLPPPP!

At the sound, I snap to my feet and turn towards the O'Connor house.

BLLLLPPPPP!

Ignoring my glare, Mrs. O'Connor's son intently tries to get his lawnmower started again.

BLLLLPPPP!!! DROOOONE!

He resumes his march up and down the yard with the lawnmower proudly leading his way.

All around me, I can hear the lawnmowers starting up and again, an infernal chorus of **BLLLPPPPSS!** and **DROOOONES!** In-law after in-law resumes his lonely march. No one gives me another look.

Defeated but unashamed, I walk back to my house. I step inside and close the door behind me. Lock one, lock two, lock three. On TV, Mr. P is teaching Jackson why its okay for everyone to march to his own drummer as long as there's a laugh track involved. I can barely hear over the lawn mowers outside.

Someone's going to have to fix that window. I'll ask Mrs. O'Connor's son later. Maybe he'll do it for a cookie.

CRISWELL WAS RIGHT

Charles King was born in the back room of a mortuary in Indiana. He was born long ago in the past and he lived his life in, what was, for him, the present. But his mind — his mind saw only the future. Charles King would become better known as Criswell.

Criswell was the author of the widely-read daily column, "Criswell Speaks," in which he predicted the future, often times to be laughed at only to be viewed in awe as even his most outlandish predictions came true. Criswell had many talents — along with seeing the future, he was an acclaimed actor who appeared in the films *Plan 9 From Outer Space* and *Orgy of the Dead.*

Though death came to this great man in 1982, his words and his vision live on. Criswell's predictions have been proven correct 87% per cent of the time — a little less than always but a lot more than often.

Criswell predicted that by 1980, we would be able to perform our own home face-lifts for only $5.00 a pop.

Criswell was right!

Today thousands of bored housewives lift their faces and the faces of their friends for fun and profit.

Criswell predicted that nudism would become more popular in the United States of American and that, in 1971, the Supreme Court would rule that no state may outlaw public nudity.

Criswell was right!

Thanks to Blackwell vs. State of Alabama decision of 1971, we are all free to be you and me without getting hassled by da man.

Criswell predicted that, on August 9, 1970, a woman would assassinate Fidel Castro

Again, Criswell was correct.

After failing to kill Andy Warhol in 1968, Edie Sedgwick caught the first flight to Havana where she become one of Castro's Supercommies until that fateful day in 1970 when she turned against her mentor.

Criswell predicted paste-on bikinis for girls and clamp-on bikinis for boys.

Again, Criswell was correct.

Paste-ons are currently all the rage in France though clamp-ons were largely rejected after the impotency scare of '84.

Criswell predicted that the teeming metropolis of Denver, Colorado would be destroyed on June 13th, 1989 by a pressure from outer space that would cause all solids to turn into a jelly-like mass.

Sadly, Criswell was correct.

Let us all take a moment of silence to pay respect for the dead of Denver.

And lastly, Criswell predicted that the final day of life on the Earth would be on August 18, 1999, at which point a black rainbow will stretch across the sky.

And this rainbow, through forces that mankind can not begin to comprehend, will suck away our precious oxygen, causing all human civilization, as we know it, to die out.

Until the end, we can only hope and look to the sky.

Imagine if you will, millions of years from now when Carbon Dioxide organisms have evolved into the dominant form of life.

Imagine them sifting through the rubble of our ruins, much as we sifted through the remains of the Roman Empire, itself destroyed by forces it could not begin to comprehend.

Imagine their surprise as they wonder, what was a Henry Ford? Imagine as they wonder what a Hollywood was and what, in heaven's name, was a Criswell?

MARCH 3ᴿᴰ, 1992

Tonight, Jessica and I went to BPU's lyceum to see a show starring Anthony Zerbe and Roscoe Lee Browne, two character actors that no one other than me seems to have heard of. First saw Zerbe in the early '80s when he played Pilate in a silly TV miniseries called *A.D.* Browne, I knew from when he guest starred on several of the more preachy episodes of *The Cosby Show.* Apparently, they've been touring campuses around the country for the past few decades doing this show where they basically recite poems and dramatic monologues. I think they first created this show in the '70s because mostly it dealt the horrors of war (*Viet Nam on my mind* . . . Ray Charles sings in the back of my mind). We were the only ones there. When Zerbe and Browne stepped out on stage, they both shared a cynical smirk with each other. Apparently, exposing their souls for an audience of two isn't a new experience for them. Not surprising. For all the talk about how we're attending an institute of higher learning and enlightenment, it's hard to get students to take the time to attend anything that doesn't involve a keg or a bong. Still, both did a wonderful job. Art for two is still art.

BLAZING PLAIN WOMAN

I believe it was one of those
Freezing Blazing Plain morning nights
And I was in a corner of the End of the World
Debating points of cynicism with Jordan
And watching the artistic fail to be artists
When a Blazing Plain woman came through the
front door

She walked by me
Trying to wiggle leather-clad hips
And trying to get all the guys hard
With fluttering makeup smeared eyelids
And trying to prove that she was an attractive
woman
Somewhere in the decade-long past

This woman –
She was born nowhere to nowhere people
And some day she planned to return there
This woman –
She believed she was divinely protected
By non-denominational guardian angels
Who resided in a day-glow Las Vegas Heaven
This woman –
She dreamed of doing a Menendez Brother
This woman –
She kept a rent-controlled love nest
In an apartment building decorated

With mocking signs of a scornful Zodiac
This woman –
She had once been abused
By some of the finest looking football player
In all of Texas
This woman –
She had been alive for too long
For anything she did
To matter anymore

JUNE 5TH, 2000

Last night, auditioned for *Bus Stop* at the Underground Theatre. Asked the director – missed his name but apparently he's a big deal – if *Bus Stop* wasn't just a little bit "corporate" for an organization like the Underground. He wasn't amused. Afterward, went to the Fountainhead with Ryan, Mike, Taylor, Jenna, and Jenny. Drank a lot, talked about shaking things up in Dallas. "We need a real underground!" I kept saying and everyone kept nodding even as they asked, "Charlie, how much have you had to drink?" Ended up drunk and making out with some girl who was sitting at the table behind us. Wondering what her name was. I hope it was something unique. Armenia, maybe. A mystery girl needs a mysterious name. Around two a.m., when the bouncer told us we had to leave, I tried to convince Jenny to come home with me. I can't remember if she did but since waking up this morning, I can't find my wallet.

MYSELF, THE GIRL, AND THE BASTARD FROM BRAZIL

We're sitting at a top deck table on a ship sailing the Aegean Sea. Myself, the Girl, and the Bastard from Brazil.

"Every night in Brazil," the Bastard says, "I dream of America."

"That's beautiful," the Girl replies.

"That's interesting," I point out, "because every night in Texas, I usually just dream of Cindy Crawford."

The Girl chuckles. The Bastard glares. Call that one a draw. Hell, the entire night's been a draw. We're both dressed to highlight our strengths. The Bastard's wearing white slacks and a loose, button-down blue shirt that screams out open-minded South American, free of all North American hang-ups. I've got on jeans, a denim shirt, and a Humphrey Bogart tie. I can enjoy a classic film while remaining a Southerner who knows how to treat a lady.

"In America," the Bastard says, "do you have, what-you-call, shopping malls?"

"Yes," the Girl replies.

"In my country, all life, it revolve around shopping mall. Hot date — you take girl to shopping mall. That is what families do on Sunday — they go to shopping mall. All hours of the day, you go to shopping mall. It is one place in Brazil that is safe from crime — no one commits any crime in shopping mall."

He's good. Nothing enthralls American girls quicker than BS concerning foreign countries. Except maybe BS about their own country.

"Well, in Texas, all crime revolves around the shopping mall," My drawl's as fake as his *Brrrrraaaaaziiillleee* accent.

"Really?" the Girl says, "That must be scary."

"Yeah, well, it keeps them off the streets."

The Girl's from California. Blonde hair, high cheekbones, blue eyes, straight teeth. She knows how to dress — long blue skirt slit up her thigh and a tight, baize blouse that outlines both the floral design of her brassiere and her firm nipples, erect in the cold night. However, the best thing on her body is my black jacket. I'm letting her borrow it, protection from the chilling wind. It's our link.

"I wish it was that easy to take care of crime in L.A." the Girl says.

The Bastard asks, "Crime is a problem where you come from?"

"I can't go out anymore. It's not safe."

"In Texas," I say, "when things aren't safe, we make them safe. When we pass a law, we make damn sure it's followed."

The Bastard says, "Things are not so simple in my country."

Suddenly, the Girl starts talking. I'm too busy trying to discreetly to stare at her chest to hear a word she says. The Bastard's staring straight at her tits but he can get away with it — he's from another country. Lucky bastard.

A skeletal Greek in an ill-fitting tux stops at our table and stares down at the Girl's breasts until I say, "Yeah?"

"Anything to drink?" the Greek mumbles, "Last call. It is last call. Drinks?"

"Water," the Girl says.

"White wine," the Bastard orders.

"Beer." I am a real man.

The Greek shuffles off as the Girl tells us, "I can only drink in my cabin or I'll get lightheaded."

"Do you like wine?" the Bastard asks.

"I don't drink too much."

"I only drink beer, myself," I say, "I could never get into

wine. If its alcohol, call it alcohol. Don't try to dress it up with some fancy name."

To my relief, the Girl nods. "I usually just drink beer, too. Drives my parents crazy. They only drink the best."

"You never drink wine?" the Bastard asks.

"Not really."

"You are much too pretty to waste time with beer."

"Some of the prettiest girls I know drink Michelob—" I start.

"Ah, but the beautiful girls — they drink only wine. I have some fantastic white wine in my cabin from the best shopping mall in my country. Perhaps later you will come and let me show you."

The Girl's cheeks turn crimson. The Bastard smirks at me again and says, "Do you like Gloria Zedillo? She sing song, *Dance all Night.*"

Dance All Night is a bland little ditty about dancing all night. It's the song that's managed to infect all of the radio stations back in the states and one of the many pleasures of being abroad is that I don't have to hear that song.

"I love that song," the Girl says and suddenly, she's not quite as hot as she was before. Quickly, I scan the rest of the deck but seeing only a collection of middle-aged, gawking retirees, I return my attention to the girl and try not to think about her musical tastes.

"Well, Gloria Zedillo, she is from Brazil," the Bastard says.

"Really?" The Girl looks surprised. "I thought she was Mexican."

"So did I," I chime in though I have no idea.

"No, she live up the street from me," the Bastard says, "I carry her packages home from shopping mall."

The Girl says, "That's amazing."

"Some time, maybe over wine at my cabin, I tell you about her—"

"Well," I interrupt, "do you know Frank Sinatra?"

"Yeah," the Girl replies.

"He was from Texas."

"Really?"

"Austin, Texas."

"I didn't know that."

"Hardly anyone does. But he's as much from Texas as Gloria Zedillo is from Brazil." I look over at the Bastard. He's still smiling. "Yes, I read his family come from Texas." The Greek comes back with our drinks. I gulp down my beer, the Bastard sips his wine, and the Girl stares down at her water in silence. We both stare at her, trying to figure out what could be going on in her mind. Wondering if she's thinking about the Bastard or the Greek or her parents drinking only the best or me? Crime, shopping malls, sex, what?

Finally, she looks up at me. Her eyes — I notice for the first time that they're green and not blue — are somber and exhausted and they tear into my soul. She has been thinking about crime, shopping malls, sex, and parents who drink only the best. The Girl's been thinking this entire night.

She drinks her water as quickly as I drank my beer. My fate's sealed. No American girl goes to a foreign country to date an American boy. When the Bastard asks if she wants to try his wine in his cabin, I don't protest.

I'm silent as they stand and let me know it was a pleasure. And as I watch them go down the stairs to the lower decks, I smile. She'll be back.

She's still wearing my jacket.

OCTOBER 3RD, 1994

So, Jessica didn't show up for lunch today. After waiting an hour, I finally gave her a call and she said she'd only eat with me if I agreed to renounce the Republican party and send a check to Ralph Nader by November. I, of course, refused and she hung up on me. I ate alone and then wandered across campus. Saw some graffiti at the Art Building – "Anonomous God, Psuedo-King," which annoyed me both with its misspellings and just the pure stupidity of the statement. Before I could properly deface it, however, I heard a woman shouting my name. I turned around and it was one of my best friends from high school, Holly Bender. I hadn't seen her since graduation ("See you later," I said five years ago) and turns out that she's been going to the same college as me, living in the same apartments at me, for the last four years but we never ran into each other until now. Anyway, she's a Business major and she's decided she wants to be a standup comedian or maybe a child psychologist. "And you're a business major?" I said. "Yeah," she smiled, "I need to change that." Anyway, we went back to her apartment and talked about high school and where everyone was now (and discovered we had no idea where any of our former friends were). We talked about Kurt Cobain and Holly called him a "cowardly little shit." "When I tried to kill myself," she told me, "at least I did it in private." Somehow, the conversation turned to the fact that we both had huge crushes on each other in the tenth grade and, long story short, I kind of ended up cheating on Jessica. I'm trying to feel bad about that but the truth of the matter is, I don't. Holly thinks Ralph Nader's a boring fraud, too.

AFTER THE PLAY . . .

I once had a small role in a play about a murder in a small English town at the turn of the 19th Century. Now, what a bunch of shit-talking, 20th Century Texans were doing playing Cockney murder suspects will always leave me disturbed. However, what I remember most was one of the stage hands (his name was Bart Malleo, I think) telling me about how he was an extra in some recent movie where Steve Martin was a faith healer who somehow ended up fucking Debra Winger (lucky bastard). Anyway, they made the film outside Lumperkin, Texas and during the filming, a UFO flew up and beamed him up (Bart, not Steve Martin. No accounting for taste).

Each night, I was privilege to more details of Bart's close encounter. The aliens asked him what war was and Bart replied that it was an old black-and-white TV show from the 1970s that starred Vic Morrow and showed up on the Nostalgia Channel upon occasion.

"I think you mean *Combat*, Bart," I corrected him, "And it was from the '50s."

"Yeah, I know," Bart nodded, his dandruff-flaked locks falling over his forehead, "It was misinformation, you see."

Finally, on our closing night, his face turned red as he told me that he was subjected to regular anal probes by the aliens. "I ain't no sissy boy or nothing," he whispered, "but just between friends, I kinda liked it." Anyway, after that, they sent him back to Earth and he spent his days (except when he was auditioning or doing extra work) like Roy Thinnes on *The Invaders*, vainly trying to warn people about the upcoming take over of our planet by, what he called, "faggots from outer space."

Last I heard, after the play, Bart moved up to Waco and got arrested smoking hash somewhere near the ruins of that old compound they got out there. He's in jail now but still writes notes to the play's leading lady (who, to be honest, he kinda used to stalk but who didn't?). She tells me that they're very friendly, sweet notes that smell like lilacs and usually end with:

Enjoying Prison a Little Too Much,
Bart

DICKIE ECKLUND OF LOWELL, MASS

Last night Mike Tyson struck a blow
For rapists everywhere
When he took Peter McNeely down
Or came close enough
After 92 or so seconds
Of preplanned fixed glory
And I thought of Dickie Ecklund

Dickie Ecklund of Lowell, Mass
The home and destruction
Of Sal Paradise, Ray Smith, and Jack Dulouz
I thought of unstable Dickie Ecklund
Who once starred on HBO
I thought of inarticulate Dickie Ecklund
Who once fought Sugar Ray Leonard
I thought of toothless Dickie Ecklund
Living with his mother and raising his son and worrying
his nephew
I thought of imprisoned Dickie Ecklund
Taking his strength from a Sprite bottle-cum-crack pipe
Dickie Ecklund who would have become both
Pre-enlightened Norman Mailer and pre-doomed Jack
Kerouac
Dickie Ecklund who should have been
Gerry Cooney if Cooney could fight
Dickie Ecklund who would have stopped

Mike, Buster, Evander, and Riddick
Dickie Ecklund who would have rendered unneeded
Tommy Morrison
Dickie Ecklund who would have even blocked
Mighty George Foreman
I thought of Dickie Ecklund
The champion of the world
Dreaming of a crackhouse
In a prison cell
Somewhere in New England

APRIL 5TH, 1997

Later, Jessica came by the apartment while I was watching Boxing on some cable station I didn't even know I had. At first, she tried to get me to change the station and rolled her eyes when I did my best to explain the inherent beauty of boxing and become Norman Mailer. Then, a pre-fight interview with Lennox Lewis came on the TV and Jessica said, with a half-satiric girlish squeal, "He is a handsome black man!" Just like that; sex intruded on the senseless violence. After that, she wouldn't let me change the station, even though I now had zero desire to watch.

A NIGHT IN THE LIFE OF WARREN AACKLAND

Okay, he was standing at the front door. He'd managed to get out of his new Jaguar and walk up the front steps. Now, all he had to do was knock. No, no, he would ring the doorbell. After all, let's say the Greens weren't in the living room. What if they were upstairs or in the kitchen or something? It could happen. More than probable when you get right down to it. They wouldn't be able to hear him knocking. Which would mean that no one would answer and then Warren Aackland could return to his nice, cozy home. So, he'd ring the doorbell. He was a bloody professional, after all. A lawyer and a good one. Not a great one but a good one. Well, maybe not a good one when you got right down to it. Pretty damn mediocre, in fact. But he was still a professional attorney and he knew the thing to do was to ring that doorbell. Wherever the Greens were in that house, they'd hear the doorbell. And the door – the big Oak monstrosity that was supposed to bring a touch of class to the Green Home – that door would open and Warren would be staring down the barrel of a shotgun. Behind the shotgun, Jesse James Green would say, "Aackland, just what the fuck do you think you've been doing with my daughter?"

BANG!

Oh, how bloody pathetic! Warren thought. Though he was as much of a Texan as anyone else in Glory Hole, his thoughts were always formed with an English accent. He didn't really like the English all that much – except for Julie Christie who was quite the bird in her younger days – but for some reason, he thought in their voice. Or at least he assumed it was their voice. Having never been to England, he had go on a lot of second-hand information. *I'm his lawyer, that's the only reason he called me. He couldn't possibly know about me and Elaine! Anyway, what's wrong with a good snog!? She's only thirteen years younger than me! Bloody Hell!*

Of course, he was only twenty-nine himself.

Warren glanced back at his Jag. He had left the engine on, just in case he had to make a quick escape. Just in case Jesse had somehow found out.

You're a bloody idiot, Aackland! How could he have found out!? Elaine's not stupid! And you certainly didn't tell him! How could he possibly know anything!?

Warren forced his finger towards the doorbell but froze right before making contact. What if Jesse had found out? What if he and Elaine hadn't been as clever as they thought? What if. . . ?

It had been two weeks after his divorce. That's when he was first hired by Jesse James Green; owner of Green's Appliance Rental and one of the higher rungs on Glory Hole's social ladder. Everyone knew the Green Appliance jingle that ended every commercial. *Green's – Its Fast and Easy/Green's – Its Everything You Need/Green's!* At the local high school, the boys sang that jingle whenever they saw Elaine walking through the hallways in her short little cheerleader's skirt. God, Warren was seeing a cheerleader. He'd spent his entire life dreaming of dating a cheerleader! *Better late than never, right, old boy?*

Warren looked down at his finger, hovering in front of the doorbell.

You're bloody pathetic. Ring the damn bell!

The finger moved closer.

So, Aackland, I hear you've been getting blowjobs from my little girl.

The finger stopped.

Dammit, man, ring the bell! How could that redneck possibly know!?

In one swift action, the finger hit the bell.

DING—

Oh hell—

—DONG!

—what have I done?

The door opened. Warren closed his eyes, expecting to hear the rude greeting of a gunshot.

"Warren," he heard Jesse's powerful voice boom, "what the Hell are you doing!?"

Warren slowly opened his eyes to see Jesse James Green standing in the doorway. Jesse was your typical short, somewhat runty looking little man with a loud voice. His dark black hair – the gray dyed out – sat on his head like a shiny helmet and was reputedly so stiff that it could deflect bullets. His dark eyes – surrounded by a layer of brown scar tissue – coldly studied Warren Aackland. Jesse was wearing tan pants, a white, leather belt, and a dark blue shirt. A plaid suit jacket hung over his shoulders and around his neck was draped an undone paisley tie.

"I asked you what you were doing," Jesse repeated.

Hoping you wouldn't kill me, sir. "I was meditating, sir," Warren replied.

"Oh. Is that what you lawyers do now?"

"Amongst other things, sir."

"I see. Well, don't stand there letting the bugs in. Come on in."

Jesse stepped to the side and allowed Warren to enter the house. The Green living room was a cavernous space with wood paneling and a mahogany floor. The brown-furred skin of a dead bear – its head still attached with a mouth open in outrage – lay across the floor as a rug. Spread almost randomly across the room was a wide-screen TV, a white leather couch still wrapped in plastic, and gold-plated trophies announcing Jesse to be the Businessman of the Year according to the Glory Hole Chamber of Commerce. The walls were decorated with faded paintings of desert scenes and stern looking Indian chiefs. The living room stood as a testament to how Jesse James Green – the country dynamo with a booming business and a sixth grade education – felt the rich should live.

"Sit down, Warren," Jesse said.

That was a good sign. Jesse was using Warren's first name. His voice may have been gruff but that was just Jesse. No, if he knew about Elaine – well, he wouldn't be using first names. That was, at least, one thing Warren could be sure of.

Warren sat down on the couch. The TV was on, turned to some cable station. On the screen, Jeremy Irons was making faces at Melanie Griffith while Dominique Swain's teenage breasts occasionally bounced by. Warren had to repress a smile as he recognized the film. *Lolita.* The new version. Terrible, terrible movie. Warren preferred Kubrick's original even if Melanie Griffith did have a cuter ass than Shelly Winters. But Sue Lyon – God, the crush he had on Sue Lyon. Of course, that film was made a few years before he was born. Who knew what Sue Lyon looked like now? Probably a bit like Melanie Griffith—

"I have to repossess a TV from some hick family," Jesse said.

Repossession. Jesse loved repossession. Everyone had their own ways to find solace. Some went to church. And usually while they were out worshipping, Jesse was sneaking into their houses and detaching their air conditioners.

"The wife doesn't want to go tonight," Jesse continued, "and Elaine's got a date in Dallas, so it looks like you're going to be coming with me. I like to have witnesses for this sort of thing and I figure you can toss in some legal mumbo jumbo if anyone objects. Okay?"

Warren didn't hear the last part of what Jesse had said. *Elaine's on a date!? With who!? Bloody Hell—*

"Is that okay, Aackland?" Jesse's voice interrupted his thoughts. *No, it is not okay!!* "Yes, of course. Whatever you say, Mr. Green." *Elaine has a date!? A bloody date with somebody other than me!?*

"We'll go after I get the little woman to tie my tie," Jesse said.

Jesse left the living room but Warren hardly noticed. He looked over at the TV in time to see Jeremy Irons shooting a naked Frank Langella in the back. *A hick family, he said. Yeah, right. He probably just wants to take me some place isolated so he can shoot me without making a mess in the bloody living room. Elaine has a date!?* Oh, he could see them. Down in Dallas, Elaine looking beautiful and luscious with some stupid high school jock. Captain of the Football Team, probably. Some big blonde Scandinavian with his letter jacket and his dumb laugh and his Ivy League football scholarship—

Jesse reentered the room, holding the still undone tie in his clutched fist. "Warren," he said, "you know how to tie a tie?"

"Yes, sir," Warren replied, standing up and taking the tie from Jesse.

"Help me out here. My wife's gone all arthritic on me."

Standing less than inch from Jesse's bulldog face, Warren carefully wrapped the tie around his employer's neck. As he struggled to create a proper knot, he suddenly realized that he had Jesse in a rare vulnerable position. With just one quick motion, Warren could turn that ugly tie into a noose and take care of at least half of his problems—

"I checked out this guy Elaine's out with tonight," Jesse suddenly said, "Made sure he was a man of good character."

"And," Warren asked, trying to keep his voice calm and unemotional, "what did you find out, sir?"

"He ain't going to be my son-in-law but I'm not going to have to put a pound of buckshot in his ass either," Jesse said, "You don't have any children, do you, Warren?"

Well, there was that one down in Austin but Warren had his doubts about the actual truth of that and besides, he was just a poor lawyer in a small hick town. He couldn't have paid child support even if he was sure the kid actually was his. Still trying to shape the perfect Windsor knot, Warren said, "No, sir, I don't."

"You gotta watch them," Jesse said, "My Elaine – she's an angel but she's a teenager too, you understand what I'm getting at? Last weekend, whoever she was out with – he got her so drunk that she was up all Sunday throwing up. Wife had to clean all that up until her arthritis kicked in. Then I had to go bring in the dogs and lit them lick it up. Pit bulls get a bad name but they'll eat any damn thing," Jesse laughed at the thought of his twenty or so teeth-baring pit bulls licking up his daughter's hung over puke before continuing, "Elaine won't tell me who she was out with. She knows that if I ever found that guy, I'd blow his head clear off."

Oh would you? Warren thought. *Blow his bloody head clear off, would you? Well, for his sake, let's hope you never find him, shall we?*

"Maybe," Warren said, "he told her she shouldn't drink and she did it anyway just to put him in his place."

"Warren, you and I both know that there's only two type of men who try to keep a young girl from getting drunk," Jesse said, "Fags and queers." Suddenly, he roughly shoved Warren's hands away from his throat. Stepping back, Jesse ripped the tie from his neck and tossed it onto the bear rug. "Shit, Warren, you're standing too close to me. Looked like you were about to kiss me or something!"

"Uh—" Warren didn't know how to respond, "Well, I wasn't—"

"This ain't suit and tie work anyway," Jesse said, "C'mon. Let's roll. That you're car sitting out there?"

"Yes, sir, it is—"

"Great. We'll take it. It'll impress those hicks."

"Well—" Warren laughed nervously, "See, I just got it and—"

"Well," Jesse grinned, "this'll be a chance to pop its cherry, won't it? Now, let's go rescue my Sony."

*   *   *

At 8:00 PM, Warren was driving his brand new Jaguar down a dirt road. He could hear the constant *ping* of small rocks scratching up the sides of his car and a thick cloud of dust swirled around his headlights.

"Real nice car, Warren," Jesse said, "real nice."

Not anymore, you bloody idiot.

"Turn onto the next road. First farm on the right. The McIntyres," Jesse released a deep, guttural laugh from the pit of his stomach. "Those bastards. Thought they could take my TV without paying. Gonna show them, ain't we, Aackland?"

"Yes, we sure are, sir. So, anyway, who's this guy your daughter's going out with?" *Oh yes, Warren, that was real bloody smooth!*

"I got his name written down somewhere. Elaine doesn't tell me much about her love life. Guess because I'm her Daddy. She's been going out with some guy every Friday for the last four months and she's yet to even tell me his name. Except for when she got drunk. She said that was some other guy."

"Oh. Well, that's good."

"I don't worry all that much about her," Jesse continued, "Her brothers – I had to give them a whuppin' a time or two but not my Elaine. She's an angel. A perfect, little angel. Other parents got to worry about drugs and sex and gangbanging and all that other shit but not me."

"I'm happy for you." *Are you bloody blind, you idiot!?*

"But once I find that guy she was out with last Friday – I was none too happy when she came home sick, let me tell you. I swear, when I catch that guy – let's just say I'm going to show him less mercy than the McIntyres."

"But, if you don't know his name—"

Suddenly, Jesse shouted, "You're about to miss the turn, goddammit!"

Warren quickly turned the steering wheel and the Jaguar

roughly swerved down an even dark dirt road, leaving a cloud of dust billowing behind.

"Watch out for the goddamn farm!" Jesse snapped, "We don't want to get lost out here!"

"I'm sorry, sir."

"All right, I'm a forgiving man. Just don't let it happen again. Anyway, you gotta understand something about me, Warren. I didn't get where I am by giving up. I've got friends. I got friends that got friends that got friends, if you follow. And once they find this guy – let's just say I might need you at a murder one trial," Jesse laughed.

At that moment, Warren made a decision. Absolutely no one knew he was seeing Elaine. They never went anywhere local. They always drove out to Dallas on Friday night. They were safe for now but if anyone ever did find out, Warren was dead. No matter how much Elaine possessed his thoughts, it was getting too dangerous. Warren may have even loved Elaine but he loved one thing more. Himself. Tonight, when they got back to the Green House, he'd wait around for Elaine to get back from her little jock date. He'd take her to the side and gently (of course!) break it off. They would both suffer but in the long run, it was for the best.

And what if she tells her Dad? No, Elaine would never betray me like that. She wasn't that type of girl.

"There's the farm!" Jesse was yelling again, "Goddammit, Aackland, this is the last time I ever drive with you! You can't keep your eyes on the goddamn road, can you!?"

Warren brought the car to a stop beside a small, wooden house that looked more like an oversized shack than an actual home.

"Let's have some fun," Jesse said as he got out of the Jaguar.

Warren followed, leaving the engine running as he had before. He stopped to look at his car. The previously sterling paintjob was now covered in dust and he could make out long scratches running across the doors. Warren glared over at Jesse who was standing in front of the shack. *Damn you, you bloody malignancy on the face of mankind! First you destroy my love life – now you scratch up my BRAND NEW JAGUAR!*

Warren walked over to Jesse just as Jesse's voice boomed, "McIntyre, open this door immediately and relinquish what you have taken from me!" He glanced over at Warren and, raising his eyebrows, said, "Neat, huh?"

The sound of someone hocking up a glob of spit came from inside the shack. Suddenly, what appeared to be a door was thrown open. There was a loud crack and the door fell to the ground.

In the doorway stood a gigantic man wearing overalls and holding a shotgun. He glared at them as his jaws intensely chewed. The clacking of his molars echoed through the night.

"McIntyre?" Jesse said.

"He's got a bloody gun," Warren muttered.

"What do you want?" McIntyre asked, his voice a growl.

"I want my TV," Jesse said, "I want the Sony you've stolen from me."

"Come in," McIntyre said.

Jesse followed McIntyre into the shack. Warren considered making a run for his jaguar when he heard Jesse shout, "Warren, get in here, goddammit!"

Warren reluctantly entered the shack.

Like the Green House, the McIntyre House's first room was a living room. Unlike the Green House, the living room appeared to *be* the McIntyre house. The medium-sized room had one small couch (with springs jaggedly protruding), a few small, wooden chairs, two small beds, an even smaller dinner table, and a dozen or so sleeping bags strewn across the floor. Oh yes, and in the far corner, was a band spanking new, showroom quality television that was apparently tuned to – what the Hell were they watching!? Warren squinted at the image and recognized it from his college days when he actually thought he might be President someday. Was it possible that they had interrupted the

McIntyre Family as they watched C-Span!? A well-dressed man that Warren vaguely recognized as a Congressman was standing in front of a podium and giving a speech on campaign finance reform.

McIntyre stood defiantly before them and at his side was a woman who was apparently very pregnant or just very fat. A scowl decorated her face while a 12-gauge rifle lay across her crossed arms. Seven or so children – the oldest appeared to be ten – were gathered around their legs with the cherubic looks of evil urchins. And standing beside McIntyre was a young man of about sixteen (Elaine's age, Warren reflected). Even taller than McIntyre, this young man held a shotgun in his right hand and in his left was what Warren recognized as a Smith and Wesson handgun. (Warren knew this courtesy of a youthful admiration for the Dirty Harry films of Clint Eastwood.) Like his mother, the young man was scowling. His face was covered with deep scars that obviously weren't the result of poor skin care.

"This is my son, Bulie," McIntyre's voice was flat, "He got the TV. Bulie, did you get the TV from this man?"

McIntyre pointed to Jesse who was standing in the middle of the room, smirking. Warren attempted to hide behind his boss and realized he was starting to fearfully sweat. The little urchins were all staring up at him and Warren remembered how much he hated kids.

"Yep," Bulie, the scarred 16 year-old, replied.

"And you didn't pay me my rent," Jesse said, "Therefore, it is my sad duty to repossess it. Mr. Aackland here – Warren, get out from behind me! – is my lawyer. He'll answer any questions. He's better with that legal stuff than I am." Jesse continued to smirk, "Too many big words for me."

"What do you mean repossess?" McIntyre asked.

Trying not to stutter, Warren replied, "We're taking it back."

"We bought it."

"No, you rented it," Jesse said, "Its Green's Appliance Rental, not Green's Appliance Seller. So, hurry up and get it out to the car and let's get on with this. Okay, good buddy?"

McIntyre shook his head. "You can't have it."

Jesse laughed. "What?"

"You heard me. We need that TV."

"Mr. Aackland, explain to these good folks—"

"Nothing to explain," McIntyre cut him off, "C-Span. Business of the country. My wife loves it. Bulie loves it. My kids love it. I love it. Maybe when Congress goes on recess, you can borrow it. But you ain't taking our TV until then and that's all there is to it."

"You should of thought about that before you stopped paying," Jesse said.

"Went send all our money to Tom Bradford to help pay for his kids education. He's got eight of them."

"Tom Bradford?" Jesse said. He glanced back at Warren and muttered, "Who the Hell's—"

"He's the father on *Eight is Enough*," Warren explained.

"Eight is what?"

"Its an old TV show. Maybe they show it on C-Span now," Warren shrugged.

"Well, take care of this Mr. Attorney," Jesse said before turning back to McIntyre. "I've consulted with my lawyer. Warren, go ahead."

Warren cleared his throat. He could hear the Jag's engine purring outside. "Mr. McIntyre," he said in his best cross examination voice, "am I to understand that you send all of your money to a fictional TV character to pay for his fictional children's fictional education?"

"Yep," McIntyre nodded, "You ain't taking our TV."

"I'm within my rights," Jesse said, "Right, Mr. Aackland?"

"Uh, sir—"

BANG! Warren briefly saw one of the little urchins holding a smoking gun and he heard the sound of a TV screen shattering as an explosion of sparks lit up the shack. As Bulie and his parents cocked their guns, Warren lunged forward, tossing the little McIntyre demon children out of his way as he crashed into the back of the shack and another impromptu door crashed to the ground. As Warren leapt out of the shack, he heard more gunfire and shouting. Warren ran blindly ahead, he could hear footsteps behind him. Suddenly, his foot hit something and he crashed down to the ground in an undignified heap. He rolled over onto his back and realized he was lying in mud that was now spread across his suit. Above him, a chicken stared down quizzically.

And above the chicken, there stood Bulie. The barrel of the rifle was pointed at Warren's head while the shotgun was held down against his side, pointed at the muddy ground.

"You ain't takin' TV," Bulie said.

Bulie cocked the rifle and Warren's mind was flooded with images of Elaine. Studying for a test, doing her homework, getting drunk, or throwing up in the back seat of his car; the images pounded away at his fear. How he loved her! He had to live – just so he could love her.

Frantically, Warren felt the mud around him, desperately looking for a stone or anything. Finally, after an eternity of Bulie chuckling, Warren's hand came across an egg.

Quickly, Warren threw the egg. The white missile hit Bulie squarely in the forehead and the yoke splattered into his eyes. Blinded, Bulie screamed and pulled the rifle's trigger. Rolling to his left, Warren managed to just barely move out of the bullet's path as it smashed into the mud beside him. Warren struggled to his feet just as Bulie, blinking madly as the yoke burned his retinas, pulled the trigger again.

Warren heard the bullet whiz by his ear. Screaming in fury and pain, Bulie tossed the rifle to the ground and, using his now free hand, he ripped the yoke from his face. Seeing more eggs around his feet (along with a rather angry chicken), Warren fell to his knees and started to grab the potential missiles. The chicken immediately lunched at him, pecking its sharp beak into his hand. Screaming in pain, Warren yelled, "You bloody—"

Before he could produce a proper label for the chicken, there was another gunshot as Bulie pulled the shotgun's trigger. Just as suddenly, the chicken exploded into a mass of blood, bone, and feathers. Something stung his cheek and Warren felt a trickle of hot liquid running down his face. He was bleeding!

Warren looked up at Bulie, his eyes filled with hate. For these McIntyres, he'd very nearly lost his girlfriend, his car, and now, he was probably scarred for life! And if a lawyer didn't have the looks, he didn't have a hope with juries! Everyone knew that! He glared up at Bulie McIntyre and tried to plot his next move. But Bulie was no longer looking at him. Bulie was staring at the ground, the smoking shotgun at his side.

"BO!" Bulie suddenly yelled as it dawned on him that he had killed Bo, the McIntyre Family Chicken.

Warren took advantage of Bulie's shock to get off a few good shots. Three eggs flew through the air and they all found their targets, splattering into Bulie's tearful eyes. As Bulie screamed curses not even Warren had heard before, he staggered back blindly. Warren grabbed the rifle from the ground and rammed the butt into the back of Bulie's head, furiously praying that it would hurt and scar Bulie McIntyre as badly as he and his family had hurt and scarred Warren Aackland. As Bulie fell to the ground and lost consciousness, he said, "I'm sorry, Bo—"

Warren looked over at the shack. Through the now permanently open doorways, he could see that the shack had been plunged into darkness and he could hear more shouts and gunfire ripping through the air. Suddenly, around the side of the shack, came his BRAND NEW JAGUAR. Coming to a screeching stop in front of him, Jesse James Green triumphantly pounded on the steering wheel and yelled, "C'mon! Time to hit the road!"

Warren jumped into the passenger's side, mud and all. In his hands, he clutched the shotgun, a spoil of war. In the back seat was the television. Its screen was shattered. As Jesse pulled away from the shack, the gunfire continued to echo and Warren wondered if the McIntyres knew or cared who they were shooting.

"Well," Jesse laughed, "that was fun!"

*   *   *

Jesse continued to laugh all the way back to Glory Hole. At least a dozen times, he slugged Warren's shoulder and said, "We'll have to do that more often!"

Warren spent the trip back looking at his reflection in the rearview mirror. He had only a small scratch, just a little blood. Nothing to get worried about. Still, he wondered if it would leave a scar.

When they arrived back at the Green House, Jesse glanced down at his watch and said, "Its ten o'clock. Elaine's still not home."

Warren looked out at the empty driveway. "No, I guess she's not." After dealing with both Bulie and Bo, the thought of Mr. Quarterback only made Warren laugh.

Warren and Jesse got out of the car. "That was fun," Jesse repeated, "Have to do that more often. I know some really crazy shits we can go visit. Make the McIntyres look like a Sunday tea party, I tell you what. Oh, by the way," Jesse said, "you can keep the TV. Damn thing'll never work again."

Jesse walked to the front door. He opened the door and then turned back to Warren. The two men stood at opposite ends of the front pathway.

"If you're fucking my daughter," Jesse said, "you better hope I never find out."

He stepped into the house, closing the door behind him.

Slowly, Warren got back into his newly dented car. Jesse's words rang through his ears. Did he know? Or was that just a general threat? Maybe he was just covering his bases? But what if he did know? Was he giving Warren a chance to end it now before Jesse ended it for them? Was that his reward for bravely battling the McIntyres? Staring at himself in the rearview mirror, Warren ran all these concerns through his mind but inevitably, he came back to the same, all-important question.

"I wonder," he said, staring at his reflection, "if Elaine likes scars?"

MARCH 2ᴺᴰ, 1992

Today, in creative writing, Bill read his first story. Bill's older than the rest of us and usually keeps to himself. He's going bald, getting fat, and wears glasses so I feel an automatic kinship with him. However, he's also worn the exact same '80s Iron Maiden t-shirt to every class this semester so I'm not really sure what to make of him. Anyway, before he started, Bill said, "This is auto-biographical." He read us this long, whiny story about being a virgin at thirty-six and had us all cringing in embarrassment. Most of the class refused to believe he was actually a virgin but I couldn't believe he was only 36. Afterward, Dawn – the redhead that I always sit beside – said, "Why don't you just go to a hooker or something if its bothering you that much!?" and all the other girls in the class quickly (and vocally) agreed. Bill looked suicidal afterward – especially since he only wrote the story out of a hope that it would help him to finally get laid. I think all of the guys expected the women to feel badly for Bill and instead, they were harder on him than we were! As far as us guys are concerned, we are all now very afraid of women in general and female writers in specific.

DINNER AT CAFE BRAZIL WITH JONATHAN BELL AND JOSEPH ZITT, CONTEMPLATING THE END OF POETRY AT CLUB DADA

We're at the center table
And Joe and Jonathan have been
Sharing old memories of Jewish education
And have begun to sing off-key in Hebrew
And I'm thinking and obsessing
Over the end of poetry at Club Dada

An hour, maybe an hour and a half earlier
We had read our work
And poured out our angst
To a room filled with no one
Each of us reading to three others
Who were to busy contemplating
Which of their demons they would unleash
On their audience to care
About the words of others
Blind preaching to the blind

There will be no more Poets' Showcase
At Club Dada after this month
Because the people do not care to be an audience
And the audience doesn't care to hear
Of our petty betrayals and desires
And as I sit at Cafe Brazil
I wonder why I ever thought they should

At the table across from us
A woman sits stroking a man's hand
Because stroking anything else could mean death
And at the table by the window
A black man glares over at me
Convinced that I hate him
As surely as I'm convinced he hates me
And behind us sit two girls
I went to high school with long ago
Talking in strained whispers and giggling
I remember them jumping through the gym
Little skirts whipping above starved thighs
Working the students into a mad frenzy
As our poetry never could and never will
And I imagine them now grown-up and leading cheers
About rich girls crimes and innocent girl perversions

Outside I can see the neon of Club Dada
And I can see the bouncer
Throwing some guy wearing a Philadelphia Eagles cap
Out onto the street where the man spits up
A combination of bile and ale
And another man, thin from years of wanted abuse,
Is begging two women
Both in identical black suits
For four bucks to help buy some booze
I ain't no panhandler he explains

That's the first thing
I'm just an alcoholic and I got an addiction
The woman shrugs and hands over ten bucks
Thank you, ma'am, Jesus bless you.

Why should they care, I silently ask
As Jonathan and Joe speak of wild days in Austin
Why should they care that once we couldn't get a date
And that once our parents wouldn't let us use the car
Or that we worry about the races of the world
Annihilating each other
(If just because we might be included)
Who are we to speak of what others wish to ignore

The former cheerleaders flirt with their waiter
And leave him a quarter tip
They stand and start to walk out of Cafe Brazil
Still secure in the knowledge that they can rally the crowd
The movement of their hips is poetry in itself
Left cheek up, right cheek down
Right cheek up, left cheek down
It's like some sort of clockwork
And as they walk out the door
Every male eye in the place is on them
Except for Joe and Jonathan
Who are speaking of shared acquaintances
And I wonder who needs pretty little words
When you've got nice round ass?

COYOTES DON'T SCREAM

It always starts the same, with the sound of a coyote screaming.

Fade in:

My new boss's massive form is uncomfortably stuffed behind that fake Oak desk of his. He's dressed as always – cheap, blue slacks, short sleeve, button-down white shirt, and a clip-on tie. His bald head sits on his shoulders without the benefit of a neck. His gray eyes are dull, without a flicker of imagination behind them. On his shirt, a small nametag reads "Worthington Keeper."

"Come in," he'll say in a voice that has no accent or expression.

I'll walk into the office that seems to get wider with each step and as I approach, I'll notice that the desk is covered with back issues of *Smooth Gent Magazine*.

"You Clarke?" he asks.

"Daniel Clarke," I reply.

We've had this conversation before.

"Worthington Keeper," he says.

He shakes my hand and his grip is as bland as his voice; neither strong nor weak but just there.

He tells me that I'll be keeping the store clean and making sure everything's stocked up. He tells me the work will bore me and he's had to fire many *boys* (that's the term he uses) who thought they were too good to work for him. He asks me if I'm too good to work for Worthington Keeper.

"I'm not too good," I'll reply.

Cut to:

I'm sweeping up in back. I think I'm working in a warehouse this time – the location changes from time to time. Boxes surround me. Always boxes.

Tommy walks up to me. Tommy's twenty-three and he's going to be a great film director some day. He's carrying a newspaper.

"Another one dead," he says.

"Huh?"

"Haven't you heard? Our little town's got it's very own sexually deficient, mother-hating, closet-homosexual serial killer. You need to get out more, Clarke. It's the talk of the town. You know what's really neat?"

"What?"

"I know who the murderer is."

"Who?"

"Mr. Keeper, of course. Look in the boxes."

Tommy goes up front to check out a young blonde in a miniskirt; the type of girl who doesn't exist in this town. Tommy tells her that Worthington Keeper is the murderer. The girls grins and nods.

I lean forward and look into one of the boxes.

Empty.

I glance into the box next to it.

Empty. Still.

Cut to:

"You wanted to see me, sir?" I say as I step into the office.

Keeper looks up from the latest copy of *Smooth Gent*. "Why do you work here?"

"I needed a job."

"Why isn't a young man like yourself in school?"

"Already learned everything I needed to know."

"Why aren't you out flirting with girls?"

"I do—"

Keeper laughs a laugh as bland as his voice and grip. "No, you don't. You don't even come close. I was a lot like you once, Clarke. Dropped out of school, women wouldn't give me the time of day. Y'know how I survived? *Smooth Gent.*"

He holds up the magazine, opens it to the centerfold. I stare at 22 year-old, implanted, airbrushed, fake blonde, easily turned on, old fashioned girl Darla. "You're type?" he asks.

"Anybody's type, I guess—"

"Yeah, well, she wishes you were dead." He tosses the magazine down. His fingertips are red and blood is spreading out from the pages of *Smooth Gent*. The blood runs across the floor and laps over my shoes.

Fade out.

Fade in:

After work, I drive down to a drive-through to get some food. It's like one of those fifties diners – skating waitresses, red thunderbirds, greasers with sideburns, the whole deal. I'm sitting in my car, waiting on my order, and listening to a song on the radio. I can never tell which song it is.

That's when I see him.

He's standing a couple of spaces down from car. His thin body's covered by a suit and an overcoat – all black and blending in with the dark night. His face is long, high cheek-boned with a forehead ending in a pale shock of hair. His skin is chalky white and nearly glows. He sees me staring and smiles. His lips are dark red. I try to look away but he's already at my car.

"Hello Clarke," he says, leaning through the open window.

"Do I know you?"

"Of you know me," his voice is low and guttural, "You work for me. Worthington Keeper." He reaches in through the window and shakes my hand, nearly crushing it with his grip. "Don't you recognize me after dark?" A growled laugh emits from the deathly body, "Guess the night just does something to me. Clark, do me a favor. I need a ride."

"Where?"

"Home. Raise in it for you."

I nod. "Sure."

"Wait here."

And he's gone.

Cut to:

He's back, glowing in front of my car. In his arms, he's holding a large, black bundle. "Open the back door!" he yells.

And the back door is open. He walks up to the car, tosses the bundle in back. I turn in my seat to see what he's given me. Coats. Piled up from the floor to the top of the car, blocking out the back window. Overcoats, rain coats, leather jackets, denim jackets, suits, burly winter coats, children's coats, hundreds of coats.

"Had to stop by the cleaner's," Keeper says.

He's in the passenger's seat.

Cut to:

The road in front of us is empty. All around me is desert. I've never seen this place before.

"Where are going?" I ask.

"You ever come out here?" Keeper says.

"No . . ."

"I do. Know why?"

"Why?"

"To hunt coyotes. You ever seen one of those things up close?"

"Never."

"I have. Pure scavengers, Clarke, that's all they are. They'd kill their own for a good meal. You look in the boxes?"

"No, sir—"

"What did you see?"

"Nothing."

"You didn't look hard enough."

He's gone.

I slam down on the brakes, bringing the car to a screeching halt and I look around the car for Worthington Keeper. I'm alone. The only sound I can hear is a coyotes screaming out in the desert. Coyotes howl. Coyotes don't scream.

A drop of blood drips onto my forehead.

I look into the rearview mirror. My face is covered with blood but I'm not cut. My clothes, soaked with something, stick to my body. I stare down at my hands. They're not *my* hands. In the rearview mirror, I see a pair of vacant eyes staring at me.

I turn around in my seat. The coats are gone, replaced by thousands of bloodied heads. The heads of men, the heads of women, the heads of children; they're all tossed into a crude pile. Eyes stare at me with accusation. Mouths scream at me in rage. In the desert, a coyote screams—

Cut to:

And again, I'll look down at my fingers, caked in dry blood, and I'll realize that Worthington Keeper has sinned again.

And somewhere in my head, the coyote will scream again.

LOOKING FOR ARMENIA

She was pro-choice on abortion and she was damn proud of it. I met her in philosophy class where we debated the merits of Pascal and Chomsky and found predictable nothing answers to predictable nothing problems. I asked her for her name and I swear she said Armenia. Her mother was hippie socialist socialite and her father played drums for the Grateful Dead. Her brother was serving time in Turkey for crimes

that were invented by the state or so she claimed. She had done campaign work for Ross Perot and she feared Mother Earth was stricken. She liked to read the works of Henry David Thoreau and she spoke wistfully of nude frolic in Walden Pond. She smuggled her stash in the cups of her brassiere and assured me *Fantasia* was great "when you're stoned." She wasn't really my type but I thought her name was Armenia and how often do you find a girl named Armenia? On our first date, I analyzed the films of Orson Welles for her. On the second date, I still thought her name was unconventional and we ended up sleeping naked at my sister's apartment. On the third date I said, "I love you, Armenia." And she replied, "My name is Arlene." So, I sent Arlene away and continued to look for Armenia.

DECEMBER 9TH, 1994

Between classes, I ran into Holly. We skipped class together, had lunch at the Flying Tomato and went back to my apartment. She's decided to be a blues singer now. I showed her my latest story. She read it, laughed occasionally, and when finished, said, "You can be such a dork sometimes, Charlie, but I still love you."

AS DID HITLER

Free Mumia Abu-Jamal
Because he writes
In prison

AN OPEN LETTER TO THE GREAT WHITE AMERICAN LIBERAL

Why Mumia?
Did Danny Faulkner steal your lunch money?
Did Leonard Peltier just get too boring?
Did you just want a chance to see real-live movie stars up close?
Did it help you forget all those times you've silently spoken the N-word?
Did it excuse the wages you pay your "help?"
Did it make you feel all gooey *down there*?
Why Mumia?

Somewhere in America's crowded death rows
There sits a convicted man waiting to die
A man who didn't play Sidney Poitier to your Spencer Tracy
A man who is actually guilty of nothing more
Convicted, arrested, and condemned because he was too black

Waiting to die while you pat yourselves on the back
A man who doesn't have cool dreadlocks
A man who doesn't look like a movie star
A man who doesn't get your insides all tingly

A man who doesn't have a show on NPR
A man who doesn't have a literary agent
A man who doesn't speak in articulate tones of
moral superiority
A man who doesn't make a rich white feel like a
Black Panther

This man waits to die while you play your saintly
games
This man dies while you wait for the world to kiss
your silvery ass
This man's blood should burst from your golden
veins

REDNECK MAURY

You gotta hate Redneck Maury. As the man himself would say, "No ifs, ands, buts about it, no sirree." See, Maury's mind is incapable of much more than the most banal of statements. These are expressions he happened to hear in passing over his fifty-three years and he uses them under the full belief that they sprung from his own creative recesses. That's why you've gotta hate Redneck Maury. His mind is dull; his life is worthless.

Plus, he's evil. Maybe you doubt that but there is no moral equivalence here. There are no gray areas. No ambiguity. Redneck Maury is evil. He likes to tell people, "Now, I ain't picking on you," and he believes that. Truly does. He's a blind man with 20/20 vision.

This man, where did he spring from? A town called Glory Hole, he'll tell you. Grew up back when people were decent, back when men were willing to work. "This new generation," he'll say, "I worry about them. Don't know how to sweat. All they need is a good whuppin." That's right. Whuppin. That's how he'll say it and when he sees the smug smile of a response, he'll say, "You can laugh if you want but it don't change noth-ing."

Redneck Maury's father used to give him a good whuppin. Take him out back, whack his ass a few times with a belt. Taught Redneck Maury how to be a man, he did. Maury's got two boys of his own. Eighteen and twenty. Still living at home, living off what little money their father brings home. "You need to learn how to sweat," Redneck Maury will tell them. "Fuck off, Dad," they'll reply. "I done all I can do," is all the man can find to reply.

Redneck Maury will tell you he dropped out of school in the

second grade and he'll be telling you the truth. See, this man does not lie. This man is the most honest man you'll ever meet and some people would say that makes him a good man. Redneck Maury certainly does. "I tell it like it is," he says. He thinks he came up with that expression. You gotta hate the man. You really do.

Now, believe it or not, there is somebody who might love Redneck Maury and that would be his wife. But there are things that must be understood about that. Such as, Mrs. Redneck Maury's not all that smart. In fact, she's downright dumb. She's not one to hate. She's too nice for that. But she's not smart. She's a dumpy woman with a face that isn't quite ugly but certainly isn't attractive. She loves Redneck Maury because she thinks he's the best she can do. Redneck Maury thinks he loves her. Even when he tells her that she's worthless, he loves her. Every night he pushes his dinner aside and says, "This tastes like shit. What the fuck you been doing all day!?" Sounds a little harsh, doesn't it? "Well, I ain't picking on her," Redneck Maury says, "She's my wife. She's the mother of my kids. I love the stupid bitch. I'm just telling it like it is. See, I don't lie."

He doesn't fuck either. Redneck Maury hasn't been able to get it up for about ten years now. Not that his wife ever really enjoyed having sex with him all that much. Too much grunting, too much shoving. This used to bother Redneck Maury so much that he'd release his frustrations by slapping her or the kids around. But he admits that. "I'm a man and a man admits his mistakes," he says, "I done some bad things but I'm honest about them. Don't claim to be no saint." On his fiftieth birthday, his arthritis kicked in and Redneck Maury couldn't make a fist anymore. So now, he gets out his frustrations at work.

Yeah, Redneck Maury's still working. "Coulda retired but that sitting around – that ain't for me. I need to sweat." He's a night manager at a grocery store. Not a very good night manager, either. Everyone hates him. He gives customers the creeps. "But I get things done, nobody can't say I don't." Redneck Maury leads by yelling and reducing cashiers to tears. He's actually good at that. When Redneck Maury yells at you, he can make your name sound like a four-letter word.

Nightly store meetings are where our man shines. "Boys," he'll tell his backroom crew, "I don't use this language often but I feel that last night, you boys fucked up.. Maybe you don't think it's a big deal but you gotta understand that shit rolls downhill."

Redneck Maury's momma always told him, "Maury, Jesus forgives but people don't." Maury never understood what she was trying to say but then again, he's noticed that women say a lot of things that don't make much sense. "I don't claim to understand 'em," he says, "I just like the way they move when they walk."

Redneck Maury works the overnight shift which means he leaves for work at 10:00 PM and arrives home the next morning around nine. His wife always has his breakfast of sausage, bacon, and eggs waiting for him. And then she goes over to the nursing home to spend some time with her own mother, whose mind hasn't been there for quite some time. "Her mind ain't ever been right to begin with," Redneck Maury says, "At least now, I don't gotta listen to her yapping." On most mornings, he eats his breakfast with his two sons. He asks them what they're going to do during the day. His sons sit quietly and dream of killing him.

"You need to learn how to sweat," he tells them, "You ain't too old for me to give you a whuppin."

The boys say nothing.

"Now, and I would never use this language around your mother—" but then Redneck Maury stops talking and starts to make a really strange sound. It's a weird "ohhh . . ." coming out as a strangled groan from his constricted throat. As his sons watch, he grabs his chest and suddenly, Redneck Maury's wrinkled old face is crumpled up into pain. His features disappear into a mass of crisscrossing lines as he manages to wheeze, "Call a doctor . . . call a doctor . . ."

The boys say nothing. One of them eats his bacon while the other barely hides a smile as their father lurches back in his chair and continues to beg for them to call 911. "What's . . . wrong . . . with . . . you!?" he demands, his voice an agonized whisper. "call . . . a . . ."

And then Redneck Maury falls forward in his chair and his face plops down in his scrambled eggs. He doesn't breathe. He doesn't speak. He doesn't feel. After fifty-something years, he doesn't live.

His boys – remembering so many whuppins now – finish their breakfast and wash their plates.

"I guess we should call a doctor," the youngest says looking down at his father's body, "You better go tell Mom."

The oldest shakes his head. "You tell her. You're her favorite."

This argument goes on until the youngest goes to his parent's bedroom and searches the closet until his finds his father's gun. He returns to the kitchen and shoots the oldest dead.

He then gets the keys to his father's pickup truck and the youngest drives away. Doesn't leave a note or anything. Doesn't bother to grab any money or a change of clothes either. The youngest will probably end up regretting all of this but nobody ever accused Redneck Maury of raising smart children.

And Redneck Maury remains face down in the breakfast that he was only two minutes away from pushing away. His final, pre-cardiac arrest thoughts: *This tastes like shit. Need to teach that woman how to cook.*

Redneck Maury's dead. And you know what? You still gotta hate him.

GOIN' SOUTH

After my Dad dropped dead and my brother kinda got shot (don't know how that happened), my mom kicked me out so Meredith and I decided we were going South while there was still a South to run for. Meredith had the car, the acid-weed combo, and the contraception. I had the money, the CDs, and a lawyer's phone number. Well, the lawyer picked our pockets, the media synthesized the music, AT&T disconnected the phones, and Meredith digested the drugs and took the car on a bad trip to see Jim Morrison. And the contraception – well, you know. So I went downtown and a quest for cash. I tried to pillage a 711 with a pistol full of H2O by the clerk was thirsty that day. I advertised on lonely street corners with signs reading *If you want to have a good time, jut climb up my leg and have a ball.* No takers. I found myself a payphone and I called my Meredith and asked her if she still dreamed of the South. Her mother told me she'd gone to Hell with her brother. So I went to Texaco and pocketed a Mapsco and I had a Zima as I drew myself a blue-ink route. Maybe, maybe – maybe we should just go up North.

12 MIDNIGHT MONTGOMERY HALL LOBBY BLAZING PLAIN UNIVERSITY

I'm sitting in the lobby
Of the Montgomery Hall Dormitory
And I'm hearing this music major
Telling all the other music majors
About the awful burdens of his life
As a white
Male
Middle-class
College student

He's tall enough to duck through doorways
And he's thin enough to be bulimic
(Are there guys suffering from Bulimia
I've never seen one on CBS)
He wears his hair long and he has a goat-tee
So he can be an individual
Just like everyone else

This guy
His name is Austin

This guy is pissed off at his parents
For being his parents
This guy is pissed off at Bill Clinton
For being on TV too much
The guy is pissed off at George Bush
For being on the cover of *Time*
This guy is pissed off at everyone
Except for Pink Floyd
And on a good day
Led Zeppelin
And on a good lay
Little Austin

And Austin is telling
In his loudest voice
About his first time
To hear *Dark Side of the Moon*
It came on the radio
For there is never a time
That Pink Floyd is not playing
Somewhere

And it was like a religious experience
Like Paul on the road to Damascus
Or Joseph Smith visiting with Moroni

One of Austin's loyal apostles starts
To recount her own Pink Floyd experience
While I sit in a corner of the lobby
Playing the role of Thomas

She tells of how her parents did oppress her
As parents are known to do
And how her only solace was to be found
In a compact disk copy of *The Wall*

(!!!!THE HOLY WALL!!!!)
Austin nods for her to preach on

She listened to *The Wall* for thirty days
And thirty nights
And then her parents did come to her
And told her she was becoming obsessed
And obsessions lead to hardcore drugs
And bad Beat poetry

And she grabbed her compact disks
And she did hold them to her breast
Like a newborn
Or an underage lover
And she yelled at her parents
You've taken everything from me!
Must you take this too!?

!!!!HALLELUJAH!!!!

Austin is moved

Hell
Even I'm moved

This is Austin's final semester
Soon he'll graduate
Soon he'll have to leave the lobby
Soon Austin will be a solo artist
Just like Roger Waters
Or Robert Plant

However for now
Austin decides the time is right
To change the subject

And he starts to explain the Republican Congress
He understands it all so perfectly
Because he saw it on TV

As for me
I stay where I am
And hope for
Salvation

TWO CAR COLLISION ON HIGHWAY 61

I'm lying in my flying bed, doped out of my mind on painkillers that were prescribed by some doctor who happened to be crossing the street at the time. I'm floating through an open window and above the entrance ramp of Highway 61 where some non-tax payer named Juan is helping to scrape up what's left of her puke green Nova off of the street so that others can go to play.

She was blonde and she had blues eyes. She had boobs out to here and she had an ass that could have defrocked the Pope. She said she had to get to work and she said she had bills to pay and she said she'd see my ass in court. I told her how my day was going and I laughed at my own jokes (somebody had to). I asked her if maybe she'd be willing to just settle out of court in return for an expensive dinner followed up by a night of expert sexual intercourse at my bachelor pad.

She glared at me and I think I know what she said next. I swear I think she said something about sexual harassment (though that could just be the painkillers fucking with my memory; I'm not sure). I told her my name wasn't Clarence Thomas and she sure as Hell wasn't Anita Hill and my carnal abilities more than made up for her little Nova.

"My uncle works for the ACLU," she said, "He specializes in harassment cases when he's not springing retards off death row. Just because I'm a beautiful woman, that doesn't make me the property of any male and it doesn't give you the right to destroy my car!"

And then the cops arrived on the scene and some cracker

with a badge and a beer belly put his hand on my shoulder and told her, "You women just need to stop fiddling with your lipstick and start paying attention to the road."

I nodded and said I saw her holding a tube of Revlon up to her lips just minutes before I smashed into her. She told us we were both "Pigs!" and then got in a police car so she could get to her job as a telemarketer.

The cop asked me how I felt and I said, "Fine, except for the wave of pain running up my spine." Luckily, some guy said, "I'm a doctor!" and gave me a handful of little yellow pills. As I swallowed them, the cop grinned and said, "Pretty good shit, huh?" The doctor nodded and said, "The best, my man, the best."

And the bed is floating away from the entrance ramp of Highway 61 and back to my bedroom where the phone rings and I answer it just to be civil. Some guy from the ACLU is calling me and asking, "Is it true you made an unwanted sexual advance towards a girl named Mary?"

"Does Mary have blonde hair and a great ass?" I ask.

"Yeah," the ACLU guy replies, "and nice tits, too."

"Yeah," I say, "that's me!"

"She's suing you."

"Yeah," I say, loving my medication, "that's me!"

"She's *suing* you, buddy."

"Does she have a case?"

"Probably not but her uncle's pretty pissed off. So, you should probably send him flowers and hope for the best."

"Just send him flowers?" I ask.

"Yeah, he especially likes Orchids. Dead orchids."

"Is Mary a good lay?"

"We do not have sex at the ACLU. Have a nice day."

Click.

THE LAST ROUNDTABLE

On the last Wednesday
Of the first month of '96
Club Dada hosted the final Poet's Roundtable
As the temperature outside fell below freezing
And as slack-jawed heathens
Stopped to stare through frosted windows
And laugh at the funny men
With their silly words
Inside an audience of five friends
And seven poets
And Charlie Wax at a back table
With a flask of Southern Comfort
Came together to commemorate
The end of creative celebration
Preserved only by the mind
And a Sony cassette recorder

Joe Stanco shared memories and tales
Of being trapped with menstruating women
And crushed carnal desires
He sang the assembled a song of Dallas
And chanted of dancing on the city's grave
Jeff Ellis followed next and in slurred speech
Told of drugs, sex, and youth
And declared an inborn hatred of old poetmen
And told bizarrely personal anecdotes about noth-
ing
And as he read six poems in forty-five minutes

In the audience Jonathan Bell looked at Lea Weaver
As if to ask
How could you leave him alone with the Vodka?
And when Jeff finally caught Lea's hand signal
To shut up and sit down
Tom Stanco read several short poems
Of lust, wonder, and brilliance
Detailing all the objects in the rearview mirror
That one tends to miss
Jonathan Bell followed and declared
Even non-drug addicts like him
Could write tortured drug poetry
And the addicts in the audience agreed
As Jonathan sang the praises of crack
And all that smack
And as he spoke of former Dada annoyances
The shrieking girl, drummer boy, and longhaired
hippie freak
The shrieking girl wandered into the room
And shouted *Bad Ass, Dude!*
Joe Zitt read to us poems of a Jewish education
Solely for the benefit of Jonathan and his family
And he recounted New Year's in Austin
And revealed poems written
Under the influence of Clebo
(the great Dallas poet who didn't stop by that
night)
Lea Weaver took the stage
And read the works of others
Saying she could read her own work
But didn't particularly care to masturbate on stage
TAKE IT OFF!
Jeff shouted from somewhere
And in the end
Jerry McElveen closed out Dada

With poems of universal simplicity
Of everyday life and everyday nature
And from somewhere
TAKE IT OFF!

And with that
In the next room
The shrieking girl
Started her show

And Charlie Wax
Gone from the back
Walked down a path
unknowing

NOVEMBER 27TH, 1994

Made the mistake of going to the *Process* reading with Jessica. *Process* is one of BPU's literary magazines. Comes out every semester, edited by students in the Honors program. Jessica and most of her friends (who hate me because I smoke and eat meat) worked on this semester's issue. As usual, the magazine was filled with substandard Beat rip-offs written by the members of the Honors Department clique and as they read their poems, everyone laughed at the in-jokes and patted themselves on the back and kissed everyone else's ass. I was miserable because I couldn't say anything about how full of shit this whole thing was and Jessica was miserable because I was there. One of her friends – Abdil, I think – gave a tortured speech about how he loved to write but he wouldn't give up his own second-hand identity for his art (i.e., his failures were actually heroic). When I smirked, Jessica gave me a look and I knew, for the first time without doubt, that we weren't going to make it and our love was only hatred in disguise. Finally, Dawn, the redhead from my old creative writing class, read her poem; the last poem in this semester's edition. Dawn isn't a member of the clique so everyone was confused to see her there and didn't know whether to like her poem (dealing with her underwear; a subject I found myself suddenly very interested in) or not. Most smiled and laughed polite fake laughs and Jessica whispered to me, "We always have to put some crap in there." Myself, I discovered I was now in love with Dawn if only because she was the only person there I didn't know well enough to dislike. After two hours of tortured idealism and attempts to explain why the world was a dark, dangerous place, it was a blessing to find a poet more interested in her underwear than postmodern literary theory.

TWO NAMES IN THE SECOND PARAGRAPH

Sometimes, it seems I spend every other hour of every other day booting up my computer and checking out the headlines from the AP wire. It's strange what leaves you disturbed when you look over the incoming news. Spoiled, rich brats emulating the *faux* Rimbauds of my youth and shooting up more smack than they could possibly handle; this does not disturb me. Nor do I care about the latest musician getting gunned down after announcing that his newest CD would be entitled *Shoot Me*. You make your choices and you know the consequences. If you don't, you haven't been watching enough TV. But then, I check out the entertainment headlines and I'm troubled to discover that the little kid who starred in *Home Alone* isn't quite that little anymore. He was less than a decade old when I was graduating high school and now, he's managed to grow up. He actually existed during all those years when I was trying to convince myself I wasn't going to face another birthday after my twenty-first. I read he's become a raging drunk just like me. We were both acquiring the thirst at the same time. We both dread listening to our well-meaning friends drone on at interventions. We both spend too many nights staring at the same flask of Southern Comfort and saying, "Fuck this." His parents are readying up an axe to split him in two so they can determine who gets the rich half. I jump to the national wire and read about two 16 year-old girls in McLean, New York. Far from my Southern home, these girls are still missing but have been declared dead on the basis of "physical evidence that cannot be revealed." Apparently, if said evidence *was* revealed, every nut in the state would be turning himself in, hoping to trade a confession for a prison-cooked meal. I think about these two missing girls; dead and not even given the dignity to be recovered (if even by strangers). I stare at those names; those two individual identities. Gifts from, I assume, loving parents, those names have been reduced to two clusters of letters in the second paragraph of a mass of black, times new roman font flickering on my computer screen.

VENUS RISING

By some sort of unwritten law, all of us hard-boiled, cynical writers have a long lost love lurking around somewhere in our past. I, Charles Wax who always follows the unwritten law, experienced my long lost love/lust in Austin, Texas and her name was Miranda Lyn Gideon.

It was 1984. What else happened that year worth remembering? (Reagan creamed Mondale, of course, but there was no real drama in that.) I was in the 9th Grade; as hellish an experience as anything involving junior high school or junior high school students or junior high school teachers or junior high school anything. Any escape was truly Heaven sent.

Youth in Government was just such an escape. Sponsored by the YMCA, it was a chance for teenage losers to pretend to be adult winners. Every year, from across Texas, pimply-faced, sexually frustrated adolescents would get together in Austin and pretend to be legislators and lawmakers. For one weekend, the state capitol was turned over to us. We'd wear our best suits and stand on the floors of the actual State Senate and House. We'd elect a Speaker (usually the best-looking senior from Cleburne; they usually had the biggest delegation) and debate bills that we, ourselves, had either written or copied from someone else. Everyone of us thought that some day we'd be President and several of my fellow delegates did go on to various elective offices. Hell, we're all still young. Who knows? Perhaps even as you read this, I might be sitting in the Oval Office. If so, be aware that we start bombing in fifteen minutes. I don't mean just a few little cruise missiles. I'm talking about the big boys here and all the mushroom clouds that go with them. So, read quickly.

The first night away from the ninth grade and in Austin was a nerve-wracking experience. I had spent six claustrophobic hours in this damn bus that we'd rented from Lord knows where. Six hours spent with the other dullish, sluggish, obnoxious members of the Glory Hole delegation. Our hotel was a cheap little place (for we were from a small town with small YMCA) where the roaches got better service than the guests.

The first night had only one major event, opening ceremonies. I sat there in the House chamber – which looked like crap to my critical fourteen year-old eye – and listened as a multitude of gluttonous, boring political leaders delivered speech after speech after speech.

I was sitting at my desk and by some chance of fate, I looked over to my left and I saw her. Seated across the aisle from me, she seemed to be perfectly calm and relaxed. Even as then-Governor White exhorted us to be good citizens, she was talking and laughing with her friends while showing off rows of exquisitely white and straight teeth. The girl was a dentist's fantasy. She wasn't stunningly beautiful, not in the way preferred by some beer-guzzling idiot who wouldn't have known a major piece of right-wing social legislation from a football game. But to me, she was a great vision of beauty. She had long, perfectly textured hair; too dark to be blonde but too light to be brunette. The ambiguity was intoxicating. Her eyes were like valuable green emeralds encased by the high bone structure of her face. To me, she was a vision of beauty, like Venus rising out of the ocean in Botticelli's *Birth of Venus*. She was my own personal print of that painting (minus, of course, those annoying cherubs trying to cover her up).

I watched her in the awe of the hopelessly love struck. I was captivated with every movement of her buxom, athletic body. Sure, I was just an innocent freshman and she looked to be, at least, seventeen but in the back of my mind, I knew it could work. From different delegations, we'd be just like Romeo and Juliet. Except for the suicide part, of course.

I vaguely heard Ed Logan, the dork we'd elected Speaker, say, "Miranda Gideon of Forth Worth will now lead us in the pledge."

She stood up and I realized that this exquisite creature, this ray of sunlight, this Venus Rising was Miranda Gideon.

Her name was like a song.

She gracefully walked up to the Speaker's podium and raised her hand to her large chest, which would have excited any normal, heterosexual 9th grader. (After watching our parents – even in towns like Glory Hole – pursuing enlightenment while leaving us to "find ourselves" throughout the previous decade, we were all obsessed with breasts. Even if the girl was a total bitch who didn't give a damn about anybody but herself and who sold her favors to the highest bidder, as long as she was at least a C cup we were all madly in love. And if that seemed to be the type of shallow behavior that would have encouraged angry catcalls from the studio audience of a Norman Lear sitcom, we figured we'd earned the right not to give a damn anymore. Some of us have yet to surrender this remnant of puberty.)

She delivered the pledge with real conviction in her beautiful, singsong voice. How to describe that voice. Never has a Texas twang sounded so angelic. It was a sweetly feminine voice but not at all girly. Every other girl I knew always sounded like they were either about to break into tears or start giggling, usually at the same time. These weren't voices that you could imagine in the throes of love. But Miranda's voice *was* love. She had the entire damn pledge memorized and by the end of it, I was ready to pledge my allegiance to Miranda Gideon.

After the ceremony was over and our chaperones whisked us back to the hotel, I dreamed of her. Yeah, she'd be swept off her feet by the animal charm and magnetism of Charles Wax. Even then, I felt that there was more to me than just my thick glasses, asthmatic breathing, and inability to speak to most girls. Miranda would see that underneath my awkward shyness and unathletic frame, there was a rebel, a dangerous rogue fighting for freedom. In my dreams, she knew that "nerd" was just a label used by frightened jocks. That may sound arrogant but hey, I was Charles Wax and after I hooked up with Miranda, that would actually mean something.

That next day, the delegations split into various "standing committees" where we voted on which bills to send on to the House and Senate. My bill, forbidding Norman Lear from producing any more sitcoms, was defeated on a vote of 12-3. (The three being my own vote, the vote of a guy who arrived late and didn't know what we were voting on, and a sweet girl from Lubbock who felt sorry for me. The twelve negative votes were largely due to the fact that apparently, I was the only committee member who actually knew who Norman Lear was. Luckily, television viewers across America later did the bill's work for me.) After the committees were done, I took my seat in the back of the House. After Ed rapped the '84 legislature into order, I watched Miranda – or Randy as I called her since we were obviously so close – in action. She played the game of politics like a champion. During every debate over every bill, she was up asking questions and giving what seemed to be hundreds of wonderful speeches. That day alone, she reeled off thousands of facts and figures. Listening to her, I learned how many abortions were performed daily (quite a few), the size of the national debt (large), the number of Texans living in poverty (too many but luckily most of them were down on the Mexican border and miles away from us), and just how many Texas governors had been impeached since 1900 (one, the only statistic I remember still).

Some people did get a little irritated with her. The words "Shut up, bitch," were regularly muttered by some less charitable delegates. But I thought she was wonderful as well as beautiful. I was amazed with the powers of her knowledge until I noticed the newest copy of the *World Almanac* that Miranda and her friends spent the session passing around to each other.

The Ft. Worth delegation, second only to Cleburne in size, obviously took their pretend politics very seriously. With their crisp suits, leather brief cases, and expensive haircuts, they looked

like actual adults until you saw their faces and spotted a little
baby fat or maybe a stray pimple on someone's chin. When they
looked over at delegations from places like Glory Hole, they
always did so with a smile just on the verge of twisting into a
smirk. One could hear their thoughts. *Some day, you'll be asking
me for a job. Some day, you'll be dependent on me for your life. I
hope you've figured out how to dress yourself by then.*

Of course, in my 14 year-old way, I was envious of them.
Any group of people that acted that snotty had to have it pretty
good. Watching them, I knew they were everything I wasn't.
They were from a city instead of a small town. Their voices were
powerful, resonant, Gettysburgh Address type voices and carried
none of the country, nasal tones that rung through my ears when-
ever I opened my mouth. In Glory Hole, clothes were bought
second-hand and I knew that even as I sat on the House floor,
intoxicated by Randy, I looked like a dirty little child playing
dress up. Unlike Ft. Worth, it was always hot in Glory Hole and
I didn't own any long-sleeved dress shirts. Instead, on that day, I
was wearing a short, sleeved white shirt that was vaguely translu-
cent in the way that poor people shirts always were. My blue suit
jacket – five bucks at Goodwill – was itself to small and the bare
skin of my wrists seemed vulgar when compared to the perfectly
measured cuffs of the Ft. Worthians. Watching them, I was sure
that they probably all had constant and continual sex too! How
I wanted to be a part of them, with their perfect lives, their *World
Almanacs*, and most of all, their Miranda Gideons.

Then it happened. Up until we recessed for lunch, her speeches
had been extremely Republican and right wing; endearing her to
my own conservative heart. Then, when we recessed, I overheard
her say, "I can't believe I supported Anderson in the last election."

Good God! Anderson!? John Anderson, the same left-wing
independent bozo that my Dad had voted for because "Reagan's
too old and Carter's – well, he's Carter." Was the love of my life
a bleeding heart!? A liberal? A COMMIE!? GOOD GOD!

However, I knew that I loved Randy so much, I could ignore

her political leanings. Besides, I knew I could indoctrinate her later when we were married and stuff.

For the rest of the day, I stared at her. I probably looked like a psycho! My eyes about to pop out. My mouth hanging wide open. My tongue lying on the floor. Drool wetting my desk. Thank God she never glanced over at me.

At the end of the day's session, Speaker Logan said, "Remember the dance tonight!"

Almost immediately, a page was at my desk with a neatly folded note. In extremely neat handwriting, written on the outside:

MIRANDA LYN GIDEON

DESK #120

With the anticipation of one about to see his dreams fulfilled, I quickly unfolded the letter, nearly ripping it in half as I did so.

In the same neat handwriting:

SAVE THE LAST DANCE FOR ME

My God! Was this for real? I looked over at my Randy. She wasn't looking at me. Instead, she was pointing out some revelatory passage in the *World Almanac* to one of the Ft. Worthians.

I looked back down at the note in my shaking hands. Was this note even meant for me? Was it a joke? Was my Randy an evil, castrating bitch bent on destroying poor, love-struck freshmen such as myself? Or, much more realistically, was she just madly smitten with my great, unspoken intellectual charm? Had she sensed that my quiet shyness hid a whip-smart wit and virility that would spring forth like a sardonic tiger if only given a chance? Oh, she was smitten. She was definitely smitten.

Suddenly, a terrible thought entered my head. What if Randy hadn't sent me that note? What if one of her friends had spotted me with my tongue down on the mauve carpet and sent the note as some sort of perverted joke? I looked over at the Ft. Worthians, wondering who amongst them could be so cruel. As far as I could tell, only three of them had so much as glanced in my direction during the entire session.

First, there was W. Scott Townsend. Believe it or not, even at
the age of 18, that's the name he actually used. He was a tall,
dark-haired guy with a football player's build and a lime green
suit that he wore every session. He had given a few intelligent,
very conservative speeches that should have disqualified him from
anything so sick as destroying my heart. We were ideological
allies, for Christ's sake! However, he was a laugher, one of those
people who always seemed to find something painfully humor-
ous in every passing moment. His laugh, loud and obnoxious,
often pierced the House chamber. It was the laugh of an evil
joker. Plus there *was* that suit.

Secondly, there was Doug Brady. Short fellow with bright
red hair and terminally flushed cheeks, that's all I remember about
Doug Brady. That and his voice, soft and calmly Southern no
matter what subject he may have been discussing. In short, he
sounded like the villainous CIA agents and oilmen who have
popped up in every American thriller filmed since '63. Perhaps
unfairly, his voice proved fair reason to cast him in a similar role
in my own melodrama.

And then there was the grand plotter, the evil genius. If there
was a conspiracy brewing against me, this was the man I quickly
decided would be in charge of it. His name was Nathan Muir
and he was probably the most prominent member of that year's
session. While the rest of us were still dreaming of our eventual
political triumphs, Nathan Muir was an elected public official.
The previous November, right after his 18th birthday, Nathan
was elected Justice of the Peace. He'd run in the Republican pri-
mary against a longtime incumbent, a hubris-stricken sixty-eight
year-old plumber. Understandably, this plumber paid little at-
tention to the high school student trying to get his job and as a
result, Nathan Muir won the primary with 61% of the vote. No
Democrats had filed to run and Muir was elected unopposed.
For a few weeks, the local papers had been full of snappy head-
lines like, "New Justice Of The Peace Conducts First Marriage;
Still Too Young To Drink." Muir even did an interview with

Time where he said he planned to be President by the time he was thirty-five and claimed Richard Nixon as his favorite statesman. The article even contained a few color photos of the new Justice of the Peace, revealing a rather homely adolescent with wavy brown hair, bar-rimmed glasses, and a penchant for spotted bow ties.

Two weeks later, America forgot about him and Nathan Muir became just another Texas oddity. Except to us. To the delegates at Youth in Government, Nathan Muir was a hero who was both loved and hated in equal measure. He was certainly, according to most, the crown jewel of the Ft. Worth Delegation. And maybe, I formulated, that was his motive. Perhaps he was seeking to punish me for being the one person to pay more attention to Randy Gideon than to him. At the time, it made sense. Hell, I was fourteen. A lot of things make sense when you're fourteen.

I thought I had seen the three of them gathered around Townsend's desk, writing something. I assumed it was a speech or an amendment or something of that sort. But, instead, maybe it was the very note I was holding in my hand. Was it possible that three most conservative people in the chamber had gotten together to conspire against me, the fourth most conservative?

Oh, the humanity.

I glanced over at the three of them, clustered in the back of the chamber. None of them were watching me but I could hear Townsend's loud laugh exploding from the group. I looked back over at Randy. She had yet to look over at me.

I considered writing her a note, confirming our reservation. It'd be something really macho and obnoxious, just to make sure she understood what she was dealing with her. Something like, "Hey babe, it's waiting for you! Come for a ride! Jump on in!"

Christ, Mr. Macho Intellectual here! She'd read the note and laugh and show it all her friends and then their friends and soon there would be little xerox copies of "Hey Babe, it waiting for you! Come for a ride! Jump on in!" circulating across the Southern half of the U.S.A.

No, I'd go to that dance and sweep her right off her beautiful feet. We'd moonwalk all the way back to her hotel room.

That night, I went to the dance alone. The rest of the Glory Hole delegation remained gathered in the lobby of our hotel, watching an ancient black-and-white television. The dance was across town in the Ramada, they whined, and that was too far to walk. Besides, *the Dukes of Hazzard* was on later. So, wearing my cheap suit and unworthy see-through shirt, I ventured across Austin and entered the Ramada's ballroom by myself. A lone wolf, I thought, looking for my destiny.

And apparently, that destiny was one of standing around like an awkward idiot for a couple of hours. Silently, I slouched against the wall and watched the rest of the '84 delegates trying to figure out how the Hell you danced to Night Ranger and Rick Springfield. Glumly standing there like some crazed maniac, I saw hundreds of faces but no Randy.

I did, however, see the possible conspirators against me. Townsend, Muir, and Brady all walked into the hotel's ballroom and passed right by me. Each had a girl on their arm (Homely little Muir actually had two like some teenage Henry Kissinger). They passed right by me and I heard Townsend laughing. As I watched, Brady briefly glanced back at me and for a brief two seconds, we made eye contact. There was something there. Guilt, perhaps? Either that or fear at the sight of a grimacing stranger glaring at him.

With paranoia running through my veins, I fled the ballroom and quickly made my way through the front lobby and out the doors. Standing outside the Ramada, I stared up at the sky and, not wanting to give in to either the tears or the rage inside of me, I let out a long sigh. It was a cold night. Appropriate for what was turning out to be a pretty goddamn cold life. There was no Miranda Lyn Gideon. No moonwalk to her hotel room. No chance to discover my manhood tonight. Was it all a joke? Did Miranda or the Muir Conspiracy deliberately play with my emotions? Did they sit around and plot my destruction even as they looked up statistics in their *World Almanac?* I could just see Muir reading my Almanac entry. *Most pathetic, fourteen year-old virgin of 1984: Charles A. Wax. Born in 1969 (at least there'll be one '69 in his life) in a nowhere town to nowhere people and destined to become a nowhere person. Don't let the glasses fool you, folks! This one's as dumb as can be.*

"Ah," Justice of the Peace Muir said, "perfect."

Townsend nodded, laughed. Brady – nervous at first – finally agreed to go along with it. He was the obvious weak link. Townsend would probably have to kill him later.

But maybe – shit. Maybe I just hadn't seen her. That was possible, wasn't it? Was she still in the Ramada looking for me? Did the lack of crude, macho notes discourage her? Was she in her room right now, crying herself a river?

Yeah, that was it. She lying face down on her bed, her head buried in a pillow. Tears were pouring out of her eyes like rainwater.

Yeah, right.

As I stood there, I held myself together through my imagination. In my mind, Miranda cried so much that pretty soon her hotel room was flooded with tears. In that river of tears, she drowned. Without me, she had no desire to live. The water caused the ballroom ceiling to collapse, crushing the three members of the Muir Conspiracy. And I? I was merely standing in the background, not taking joy in all the havoc but instead pitying the waste of human folly.

Well, no – not really.

Actually, I was taking joy.

The next two days of Youth in Government went by like a far less destructive dream. Miranda continued to play the political game to perfection. I remained quiet. If I got up to speak, I knew I'd hear the snickers of the Muir Conspiracy. Miranda never sent another note or returned my stare. Never was my existence or our aborted night of passion acknowledged.

At the end of those two days, I stepped back onto our death

trap of a bus and left Austin. I never saw my Venus Rising again. Oh, over the years, I discovered a lot more Mirandas and eventually, I'd even talk to a few of them. But I always knew none of them would equal up to the mythology of the first. None of them would be Miranda Lyn Gideon.

I eventually did write a short story about her. It was called *The River Miranda* and it was about a girl named Miranda who cried a river of tears and downed three jerks named Scott, Doug, and Nathan. Over the years, it was rejected by some of the finest magazine editors in the country. After three years of receiving curt form letters, I finally placed *The River Miranda* in a manila folder and put it to the side. When I eventually left Glory Hole for college, I took the folder with me. However, by the time I stepped out onto my new home, both the folder and its contents had apparently vanished into the recesses of my Dad's car, never to be seen again.

In 1992, as you might already know, Nathan Muir was elected to the U.S. House. He was only twenty-seven and that inspired a lot of "Where-Are-They-Now" type stories in the local press. FORMER KID JUSTICE NOW KID CONGRESS-MAN was one of the more flamboyant headlines. He's not quite as ugly anymore and wears contact lenses but he hasn't given up his bow ties. Maybe you've seen him on C-Span, giving a fiery speech condemning flag burners, homosexuals, or whoever else might be annoying him that week. Or maybe you've seen him in a committee hearing, leafing through his *World Almanac* while some government expert drones on about the next century's projected levels of unemployment. If you pay real close attention, occasionally you'll see him conferring with two aides who always seem to be sitting in with the committee. You might catch Doug Brady's ruddy features and you'll certainly notice that, just as Muir loves his bow ties, W. Scott Townsend won't stop buying green jackets. You'll see them, three Ft. Worthians running the government. The only thing you won't see is Miranda Lyn Gideon. Believe me, I've looked.

Maybe Miranda was serious. Maybe I did miss my chance. I didn't know then and now, after several years of wondering, I still don't know. I *do* still have her note, though. It's old now and yellowed with age. I can't read it anymore; that careful handwriting has become just a wrinkled smudge of memory. But, I still carry it around in my wallet and I guess I'll continue to do so until its not there anymore. I've even got a copy of that painting. Botticelli's *Birth of Venus*. Venus Rising.

But its not my Venus Rising. My Venus Rising is but a memory.

FORTRESS OF SOLITUDE

After I got off work and called the family to let them know that I'd be working late, I went down to my favorite bar and who did I find sitting there but a rambling Superman? As I sat down beside him, he was drunkenly cursing Clark Kent and trying to drink his life to an end with a bottle of Kryptonite '69. Nodding a greeting at him, I ordered my usual – straight vodka. Perfect for that Iron Curtain warmth that I've heard so much about. As we drank, the Man of Steel opened up to me.

He told me about Lex Luthor ulcers and bragged about Lois Lane handjobs. He talked about smoking the best Jimmy Olson had to sell and the ethical crisis of having to smile at Perry White's constant anti-Semitic quips. "And trust me," he winked, "I always come faster than a speeding bullet. But, I don't know – is it just worthless? Somehow I just don't—"

I cut him off, "Quit bitching. I've been in love with a woman I can't stand for two years now. Bullets don't bounce off my chest. And hell, I smoke two packs of cigarettes a day. I can barely jump five feet in front of me. Much less over a building in a single bound."

Sometimes, he told me, he'd imagine that he was falling like a comet. Sometimes, he looked down over the Earth he'd sworn to protect and he just wanted to be a dead rock, breaking through the planet's atmosphere and crushing Metropolis and all the rest of the world underneath him.

"I can't write if I'm drunk," I said as I finished my Vodka, "But I can't live if I'm sober." I looked at him with his ludicrous costume and swore to myself that, superpowered or not, that freak wasn't going to win this pity party, "Y'know, if I wore blue tights and a red cape, I'd just get my ass kicked. Think about that, you *yutz*."

The Man of Steel sat quietly, obviously running my words through his head. Finally, he stood up from his barstool and shrugged, "Whatever." He left the bar and I turned on my stool in time to see him flying off, undoubtedly heading off for his private sanctuary in Antarctica. As he left for his Fortress of Solitude, I ordered another drink and remained in mine.

COMMON PEOPLE

1) Recovering

I am a recovering alcoholic, a recovering Catholic, a recovering all-around asshole son of a bitch, and a recovering dreamer. I'm barely thirty but I feel like I'm fifty (or at least I assume this is fifty that I'm feeling and not just plain laziness). I live in a nice enough house with a beautiful nineteen year-old girl who probably should be out having fun with her friends rather than dealing with a manic-depressive pill-popping writer like myself. I've been awake for four days, subsisting on a diet of Coke and twelve Dexedrine a day. (That's speed in layman's terms.) My time, I have divided between watching reruns of *Hawaii 5-0* and listening to the constant squeaking wafting from next door. (My neighbors; so in love. Their bed; so damn rusted!) Finally, this girl looks up at me with vibrant eyes that I both love and hate with an envy that can only come from too many wasted birthdays. She asks me why I never look happy and the sincerity in her voice serves as a reminder that I am not a good man. First, I crave a drink. Then I cry (or at least attempt to as it seems to be the right thing to do at the time). Finally, I go down to my computer and I create.

2) Waiting For Lefty

Zac Evans lived in the shadow of the mythical '60s, a psychedelic carnival of the imagination where college students ended an unjust war by growing their hair long and handing out flowers. Drugs opened minds and, as long as you supported all the right things, sex was easily available and always good. The only people who had to worry about sudden impotence or premature ejaculation were the greedy, war-crazed men who voted for Nixon and raped Viet Nam. Like me, Zac was born in 1969 and the mythical '60s were all we knew. Me; I believed in it until I spent one night watching both *Easy Rider* and *Billy Jack* back-to-back. Turned out the '60s were a bit too self-righteous for me. Zac never stopped believing. Zac didn't care much for movies either.

Zac was a grad student at Blazing Plain University. He came to BPU to find his beliefs and spent his undergraduate career wandering around campus with battered copies of Karl Marx in his left hand and Ayn Rand in his right. By the time he started his Master's, Marx had won out.

(Much later I discovered that while we disagreed on the validity of her politics, we both had the same opinion regarding Rand's literary abilities. As I told him one night in Colorado, I was heartened to discover, once I had finished <u>The Fountainhead</u>, that when Rand spoke not a word of English when she first came to America. "I'd hate to think," I said, "that anyone could write that badly in their native tongue." It was one of the only things Zac and I shared in common. Other than Jessica, of course.)

In the literary criticism course that Zac taught, he told his students that he was a deconstructionist. "It means I spend a lot of time talking out my ass," he explained. The students always laughed up until he assigned them to actually read Jacques Derrida. When he wasn't analyzing and destroying, Zac wrote free verse about urban decay, the horrors of war, and other atrocities he had read about. Every Monday, Zac would read his poetry at a coffeehouse called The End of the World and it was there that he first met Jessica. An English major herself, Jessica was out celebrating the end of a disastrous relationship to a possessive, arrogant jerk – namely me. She approached Zac and, sweetly pretty as always, told him how much she liked his poetry. Zac responded by saying only art could save the world and from that dangling conversation sprung a two-month courtship.

They'd go out at the end of every week. Zac wrote her poetry, gave her books to read, and when she agreed that bad things were bad he called her brilliant. On the rare occasions that she disagreed with him, Zac smiled paternally and, in the same tone of voice one would reserve for a child unwisely experimenting with electricity, explained where she had gotten her incorrect ideas. After sex, Zac assuaged her lingering Catholic guilt by assuring her that he'd happily be celibate if it meant improving the life of one stranger. As she told her friends (and they, in turn, told me), the only flaw Zac and I shared was our stridency. But at least with him, it was a case of passion and not narcissism.

Outspokenly agnostic and disgusted by the Holy Father's pro-life tendencies, Zac arranged for them to get married in front of the Student Union by a philosophy professor-cum-aspiring-pagan-priest named Kenneth Slate. (Good name if nothing else.) Jessica's family refused to come, Zac's wasn't invited, and I showed up just to cause concern. I stood in the back of the wedding party with my flask of Southern Comfort and collection of bad puns and inappropriate smirks. Zac wore jeans and a t-shirt while Jessica was decked out in her best red dress. Perhaps spotting me in back or hearing the concerned whispers circulating through the other guests, Slate declined to ask if anyone had reason to protest and instead jumped straight into, "You may now kiss the bride." When I saw their lips touch and heard the beginnings of applause, I decided to take the high road and, with all the maturity I was capable of at that time, I stuck my finger down my throat in a vain attempt to induce vomiting. When Slate announced, "The groom has a poem he would like to read," I snorted loudly and clenched my hands into fists. My untrimmed nails buried into my palms and afterward, I discovered I'd drawn my own blood; a stigmata for Zac and Jessica's wedded bliss.

3) The Education of Jessica Adams

For one brief period, her name was Jessica Adams. She knew that most people thought of her as my ex-girlfriend or the wife of Zac Evans but before she had met either of us, her name was Jessica Adams. She had lived a life separate from both of us and actually had dreams that didn't involve my writing or Zac's politics. Jessica wanted to be a historian. When we first started going out, she used to tell me about her favorite, bittersweet vision of the past. In the mid-19th Century, Calvary soldiers would spend months at a time away from home and family, consumed with the endless task of killing various Indian tribes. During this month, their wives would be left alone at the fort; abandoned in a desolate wilderness with no way of knowing if their husband was returning home or lying dead and scalped three states over. To pass the time, these women would gather at nearby railroad tracks and watch the train go by. "Just so they could see different faces at the windows," Jessica told me, "Just so they could be reminded that there was something else out there beyond the forts and the plains." She'd tell that story with the awed voice of someone who believed they had just looked into the face of God. Some nights, I can close my eyes and still imagine those dowdy women, hoopskirts rustling up from their ankles as the train roars by. I can see the faces in the window. While the women dream of having some place to go, the faces dream of having the time to devote to something as seemingly pointless as watching a train whiz by. In my mind, the train always speeds up as it passes the women. To the women, the faces shift into one distorted blur as those individual identities are changed into a gigantic, featureless mass. It's a mass with no personality, no reason to exist other than to remind those outside that there's something better that they'll never be able to identify. As for the faces on the train, when they look out their windows, they see nothing there. The train's moving too fast for them to notice anyone standing still.

4) Bus Stop

If you believed Zac Evans, real Americans were to be found in Greyhound bus stations. It was there, he told Jessica, that the common man truly came to gather and if there ever was a true working class revolution, it would begin in bus stations and cheap diners. ("Indigestion," I said to him one night, "the driving force of history.") The "common man" couldn't afford a car or a fancy, gourmet dinner. He told her this as they sat in a Dallas bus station. They were waiting for a bus to Denver where they planned to spend their honeymoon.

Jessica smiled and spoke with a newlywed flirtatiousness, "So, what are you saying, Mr. Evans? That the rich aren't Americans?"

Zac nodded, glad to see that his wife actually understood. "Exactly. The rich don't belong to any community other than themselves."

When they boarded, Jessica said, "Let's sit in the back of the bus." When they sat down, she smiled and said she felt like maybe she should be apologizing to Rosa Parks. Zac shrugged and said, "We're not African-American. It's not our history."

5) Denver

Denver had been Jessica's idea. She was an athletic type who loved to go outdoors, camp, hike, and ski; all the things I wouldn't do because of a lethal combination of asthma and disinterest. Zac claimed to be a strong outdoorsman but he still argued quite vigorously that they should honeymoon in Mexico because it would be educational to see how the rest of the world lived. Jessica didn't want to be educated on her honeymoon and they argued for several days until finally Jessica began to cry and Zac caved in while silently cursing PMS.

Jessica had another reason for wanting to see Denver. Zac's father lived there. Again after much begging on her part, Zac agreed to show Jessica his father's home which turned out to be a four-story, white paneled mansion with neoclassical arches lining the porch and a spiked security gate circling the grounds. Zac explained that the house even had a name. *La Casa Grande* it was called. It had been built for a former spaceman-turned-U.S. Senator.

With proper disdain, Zac explained, "He was swept in with Reagan in 1980 and swept out by Iran-Contra in '86. And now," he sighed dramatically, "my father lives there. Some things never change."

Jessica couldn't find her voice as they stood across the street from the mansion. Though the closed gates, she could see a circular driveway surrounding the house. Three Mercedes – one red, one blue, one black – sat in front.

Finally, she said, "You used to live here?"

"No," Zac shook his head, "No, my Dad waited until after the divorce. He got a new house and I got my mom."

As they walked back to their hotel, Jessica said she used to dream of living in a house like that. Zac grimaced until she added that now she dreamed only of living with him.

6) Lessons

While they were in Denver, I attended a reception at BPU for a former teacher of mine, the poet Jake Ballard. Jake had just returned from serving as poet-in-residence for a small liberal arts college in Los Angeles. He told me that he had seen his first drive-by shooting and, though he couldn't get the image of it out of his mind, he could write a poem about it either. "It's trapped up there," he told me, "and I can't pull it out." He told me he was going to run for President. His first administrative act would be to set up a Department of Poetry with myself as Secretary. "We'll spread the words of Yeats, Keats, and Byron through the inner city. But we'll have to edit out all the gay stuff."

Later, we ducked out of the reception and spent the rest of the night getting drunk at a cheap lesbian bar. At one point, he leaned close to me and said, his voice a paranoid whisper, he considered himself to be a feminist. "But," he told me, "there's never been a truly great female writer. Do you know why?"

"Why?" I asked.

He was quiet for a few seconds and then, almost as if ashamed, muttered, "They've got too much to prove."

I smiled but I didn't agree. I don't believe in truly great writers period. Male or female; we've all got too much to prove.

7) PMS

A few months before Jessica and I finally broke up, I coined the term Political Moderate Syndrome; a glib way of describing the current unfortunate trend of the American electorate to glorify being an indecisive sponge as opposed to taking a firm position on either the right or the left. I'm a Republican who votes Libertarian more often than not. At the time, Jessica had decided that she was a "moderate, an independent" and my use of the term was my snide way of being self-destructive. When we first started dating, Jessica had been a liberal who quickly absorbed my own views after our first few fights. As we grew older and more distant, she moved steadily leftward. I always assumed this was mostly done to annoy me.

Zac hated the Political Moderate Syndrome as well but his main problem was with actual PMS. Jessica's period always hit her extremely hard. For one week out of every month, she would go through every emotion – anger to depression to insecurity and back again – as if the world truly had become a stage and she was determined to perform for the folks in the very back of the theater. She would lie in their bed, curled up into a fetal position, crippled by stomach cramps, and anyone foolish enough to approach put their lives at risk. Being a libertarian by nature, I quickly learned to keep out of her way and just wait for the week to end. However, for Zac, being a self-educated Marxist, waiting was not an option. He would tell her that they could conquer

whatever pain she was in. All she had to do was just start think-
ing rationally and let him work with her. Jessica would reply
with a spate of profanity. At first, Zac tried to educate her on the
fallacies of the emotions brought on by her menstrual cycle; as if
her period was just another one of their political discussions.
Eventually, even he gave up. He'd leave their apartment and sleep
in his office. Her period was the one thing he couldn't dismiss
with a quote from Marx or Noam Chomsky. He couldn't
deconstruct PMS and he hated that. Absolutely hated it.

8) Austin

A few months after the honeymoon, the Governor signed the
death warrant for Dwight Rosemond. Dwight was a former Black
Panther turned journalist who had moved down to Austin in the
early '70s. Once arriving, he promptly proceeded to gun down two
police officers and he'd been on death row ever since. While waiting
to be executed, Rosemond found enough free time to change his
name to Kwiese Fattah and to write several angry essays protesting
his innocence. Fattah's essays had popped up in just about every left-
wing periodical of note as had photographs that traditionally showed
a strikingly handsome black man sitting in a tiny cell. From that cell,
Fattah's eyes would shine with the dangerous intensity of an un-
tamed sex god held captive by an impotent society. When Fattah
became a hero and a martyr to those seeking a hero and a martyr, his
supporters were always quick to say they were fighting for justice.
Fattah was innocent, after all. It was all police brutality or whatever
he was using as an excuse this week. What went unsaid was the secret
hope that once Fattah was released, he'd repay his supporters by giv-
ing them the best fuck of their otherwise meaningless lives. At least,
that was my opinion.

Zac Evans, being a passionate believer of Fattah's noble sav-
agery, would probably disagree. One of the first things he had
done as her husband was convince Jessica that the death penalty
was immoral and wrong. "If we let them kill Kwiese Fattah,"

Zac told her, "then who will be next?" Yet, it was Jessica who ultimately decided that they should join the protestors gathered outside Fattah's prison and, as they rode the Greyhound bus down to Austin, it was Jessica who sincerely spoke of getting Fattah a new, "fair" trial. Zac was too busy worrying about test papers he still had to grade and how his chronic lateness would affect his teacher evaluations. Zac *was* glad to see Jessica becoming more of an activist but he still found himself growing jealous of her newfound zeal for justice. She had the strident enthusiasm of a new convert. It was an enthusiasm that Zac, no matter how much he denied it, knew had diminished for him with each paycheck he greedily received.

In Austin, they joined about a hundred other people in camping around the prison. Police were circled around the camp, staring impassively forward as they were taunted with cries of "Pig!" Every couple of hours, a different minor celebrity would stop by. The former star of a '70s cop show, a washed up protest singer from the '60s, a coke snorting B-film actor from the '80s; they all gave a speech about freeing Fattah, signed a few autographs, posed for a few pictures, and then headed back to their hotel. Jimmie Marshall, who used to star in the sitcom *Jackson and Mr. P* (he was Jackson), screamed, "This ain't no plantation! When will Texas get its ass out of the dark ages!?" Yes, the protestors wondered as their self-satisfaction washed through them, when indeed?

The second day of the vigil, Zac and Jessica met an older man named Dale. Tall and rail thin, Dale had a scraggly beard and long white hair that he wore in a pony tail halfway down his humped back. He was wearing jogging shorts and an old nuclear freeze t-shirt from 1984. He quickly took a liking to the young couple. He would tell them stories about Berkeley in the '60s (in the Mythical '60s, everyone spent at least a semester at Berkley). While Jessica sat spellbound by the history, Zac silently fumed that someone else was stealing his radical fire.

As night fell, the three of them passed around some weak

marijuana and Dale told them "about another Negro who stood up for himself in the South." His name was Lonny Hampton and, in the early '60s, Dale worked with him to desegregate Austin. One day, Lonny drank from a "White Only" water fountain. As a result, several rednecks tossed him into their pickup truck and proceeded to nail him to a tree. "They crucified him," Dale explained.

"That's terrible!" Jessica said.

"No," Dale shook his head, "it wasn't terrible. It was just what the movement needed. By doing that, those racists made Lonny into a hero. After we found Lonny's body, nearly a hundred white men came down from up north to help us out. We raised such an outrage that the pigs didn't have no choice but to arrest the guys that did it. They executed them, too. Or most of them, anyway. First white man to be executed for a hate crime, not that they called it that back then. But that's what it was. It was an important statement."

"They were executed?" Jessica asked as a stoned Zac stared up at the sky.

"Yeah. I was down the street having a beer when they done it, too. I cheered until they kicked me out." Dale smiled at the memory.

Even in his drug-induced haze, Zac still recognized an opportunity to reestablish himself. Quickly, he said, "How does that bring back Lonny?"

Dale shrugged. "Doesn't bring back Lonny. Just gets a few less haters off the planet."

Finally, Dale said he had to leave and the newlyweds fell asleep. The next day, with test papers still impatiently waiting, they got back on the bus and returned to BPU. As they rode back, Zac asked, "What did you think of Dale?"

Jessica was quiet for a moment before carefully replying, "He was – interesting."

"He was a hypocrite," Zac continued, "A total, fucking hypocrite."

Jessica didn't reply. However, when Fattah died a few weeks later, she cried. Zac tried to but he found he couldn't.

Later, Zac would return to Austin for completely different reasons. I would be with him this time. We went to a coffee-house where a friend of Zac's had sworn he'd seen Jessica working. When the suspect waitress turned out to just be a vague look-alike, Zac passed the time by telling me about the protest. "That's where it started," he said.

I wanted to feel sorry for the guy; I really did. He looked like Hell. But instead, I could only smirk and say, "What type of couple spends their time debating the death penalty?"

"There was nothing to debate! We both agreed or – I mean, I thought we did. She said we did."

As I looked at him, I was alarmed to notice that Zac literally seemed to be shrinking; growing smaller and less distinct with each passing day. I wanted to say something encouraging but my own combination of bitterness and withdraw allowed me to only mutter, "Kill 'em all."

9) The Truth (For Those Who Need That Sort Of Thing)

Aspiring; is there any word more horrid? As I sit here typing this, I'm envious of people who don't read or dream or think or – aspire. Myself, I've always wanted to be a writer and, in the eyes of most, until my name is on the New York Times' Best Seller List, I'll always be an aspiring writer. Zac wants to be an activist but until he's actually out there truly fighting for the common people, he'll be little more than an aspiring Marxist.

To me, aspiring has always been a sneaky little way of saying that while you may have the basics, you're still missing that certain something that makes you truly special and unique. Aspiring means uncertainty – either greatness is waiting around the corner or else you're just one of countless fools. You're wasting your life and you're not going to know if it's worth it or not until you're about to kick off. So, we play a game of pretend. We recreate ourselves as images from our ideal future; images that, more or less, come from our limited life experience. In my mind, being a writer meant becoming a larger than life, cynical romantic with a Bogart sneer, lots of women, and booze free flowing like genius. Being a writer meant being Hemingway or Fitzgerald and not the reality of spending isolated hours in front of an aging computer, getting fat off fast food, and reading snide rejection letters. Zac envisioned himself as Che Guevera, a dashing martyr who glowed with the charismatic swagger of the working man. He didn't expect to become an underpaid, overworked grad student who couldn't even handle his wife's period. Hopes, dreams, and expectations: these are dangerous things. When they're broken, nothing good can come of it.

10) Vanity

It was after Fattah was executed, long after, that Jessica finally called me and said it hurt her that we didn't get along anymore. She wanted "personal peace" and she asked if I would meet her at the End of the World, where Zac still read his poetry. "I'd like some personal piece, myself," I agreed, despite the fact that a deep part of me hated her. Jessica had been my first serious relationship. Certainly, she was the first girl I ever fell in love with. In retrospect, I was more in love with the fact that she agreed with just about everything I said. She continually praised my writing and called me a genius no matter what silly, juvenile crap I was producing at the time. When her friends made catty comments about my drinking or my refusal to talk to people who didn't interest me (basically everyone but Jessica), she would defend me with three beautiful words – "He's a writer." She helped me to believe that carrying my notebook with me wherever I went excused any antisocial behavior. When Jessica eventually started to turn against me, criticizing me as enthusiastically as those she once chastised, I considered it to be the ultimate betrayal and I swore never to speak to her again. (At the same time, I spent my days secretly wishing she'd give me a call and we'd talk like we were eighteen again.) When Jessica asked to meet me, a part of me knew I should say no. She, more than anyone, knew how to hurt me. But I was curious to see what marriage had done to her and, in my mind at least, there was always a chance for adultery.

When she stepped into the End of the World, the first thing I noticed was that her once-trademarked long hair was now severely cropped and domestic life appeared to have put a few pounds on her. She was wearing only the barest makeup and had gone from my designer label-clad girlfriend to some grungy, humorless-looking woman wearing jeans and a t-shirt. Looking at her, I silently thought *She probably looks like every other girl Zac's ever fucked.*

We got coffee and talked for a few minutes. She asked me what I was working on and I replied, "The usual," as I had been working on the same novels for the past couple of years. Jessica smiled, "Some things never change." Her tone wasn't affectionate, snide, or angry. Instead, it was condescending and I struggled to hold back my temper.

"So, do you still consider yourself to be an artist?" she asked.

"Yeah," I replied, "I do."

"That's good. But, I think you need to ask yourself something."

"What?"

"How can you, as a self-described artist, justify being a Republican?"

I stared at her, dumbfounded. "Why do I have to justify it?"

"We don't live in a vacuum," her replies, I quickly noticed, were brisk and automatic with the confidence that can only come from emptying your mind.

"My writing isn't political—"

"Art, by its definition, is political," she leaned forward, "The nature of the artist is to be—"

"Don't tell me what the nature of the artist is," I cut her off, "I'm not writing for the collective—"

"Have you ever," she leaned forward and her eyes narrowed, "actually read Karl Marx?"

"Jessica—"

"Have you?"

I glared at her. Even when things were getting close to the end, she may have criticized my plots or some fake bit of characterization but she had never before asked me to justify myself as an artist. I resented her presumptive tone, the cold, self-righteousness in her eyes. I resented the fact that her looks were slipping, that she was changing into a stranger, that she was just another walking cliché. Finally, I said, "You're young."

I stood up and walked out of the End of the World.

11) The Truth, continued

Zac Evans was fond of saying that without criticism there could be no art. When it came to literature, writing was no longer as important as what other people said about the writing. The central academic fallacy: anything written by someone with a recognizable name must be relevant because otherwise, why would this wise person have wasted the time to write it down? Marxism would work because Karl Marx said it would and if ol' Karl was wrong, then why was he a brand name? By the same token, history wasn't as important as what others said about history. Lincoln may have been a great man, after all, but all one need do is rewrite a few textbooks and suddenly he's eating Irish babies while Jonathan Swift rolls over in his grave.

Or, on a more practical level, Zac Evans may have had an uneventful upper class childhood (with the sole exception of his parent's divorce) but since he had branded his father a greedy exploiter, in Jessica's eyes, this man became truly evil. Which is why she couldn't really understand the heavy tears Zac shed when they received a phone call that his father had died of a heart attack in Denver.

They went back to Colorado for the funeral, again via Greyhound. This time, while Jessica watched the common people, Zac talked about never getting to know his Dad. In Colorado, they stayed with a few cousins in La Casa Grande and whereas she had once been amazed, Jessica now walked around the gaudy house and look at all of the material opulence with disgust. She thought of all the money (that scourge of the common people) wasted so that the late Mr. Evans could isolate himself from the forces of history. All that money could have bought someone like Fattah a new trial. Oh how it disgusted her. But what disturbed her even more was Zac's sudden inability to share her disgust.

Instead, he spent his time hanging out with his cousins. They all dressed in the same uniform of khaki slacks and knit shirts and Jessica – with her jeans, t-shirts, and lack of makeup – stuck out. The cousins would stare when she stepped into a room, the girls would whisper behind her back, all the while Zac assured his family that his wife wasn't weird or stuck up. She was just shy. One cousin commented, "She must be great in bed," and Zac smiled and winked as if he was a teenager again.

One morning, Jessica woke up to find herself alone in the guest bedroom. She called out Zac's name and, after a few minutes of silence, heard his laugh coming from outside. Wearing only a white t-shirt, she stepped out on the balcony overlooking La Casa Grande's tennis courts. On the courts, Zac and some guy she'd never seen before were playing tennis and with each serve, they would taunt each other like aging jocks playing touch football. Staring at her Marxist savior acting like a yuppie, Jessica finally yelled, "ZAC!"

Zac turned and looked up at her.

She smiled at him.

"GODDAMMIT, JESSICA!" Zac yelled, "PUT SOME CLOTHES ON!"

Jessica stepped back into the bedroom and for the first time in a long time, cried.

When it came time to return to Texas, Zac took the red Mercedes.

12) The Return

When they got back, things were different. Zac still claimed loudly to be a man of the people, a proud Marxist, but there was something missing in his declarations and both of them knew it. Whereas once they had both spent their time looking for any worthy cause to endorse, Zac was now more than likely to turn off the TV whenever the news focused on anything unpleasant.

"I just buried my father," Zac explained one night, "I'm not in the mood for more depression."

Depression and anger were just what Jessica was in the mood for and therefore, she started calling me, usually to argue about whatever had just been on TV. Usually, I had no idea what she was talking about but I'd disagree with her anyway just for a chance to pretend we had never broken up. She would call with Zac sitting beside her but he never got upset. When she finally asked why, he shrugged and said, "I trust you."

Finally, one night, he told her, "Sometimes I think the only reason I ever read Marx in the first place was to piss off my Dad."

Jessica replied, "Is that why you married me?"

"I love you."

"I didn't start reading Marx to piss off your Dad," Jessica continued, seemingly oblivious to his attempts at deflection, "In fact, your Dad really had nothing to do with it."

Zac sighed. "Are you on your period?"

Jessica stood up and went into their bedroom, slamming the door behind her. Zac breathed a sigh of relief, certain that he had his answer. Suddenly, the bedroom door reopened and Jessica poked her head out.

"No," she said, "I'm not."

She closed the door.

"Shit," Zac said.

13) The First Time

The first night Jessica didn't return home after her classes, Zac called me and asked if she was over at my place. When I told him no, he said he didn't care what had happened. "I just want to talk to my wife!" Again, I repeated that I hadn't seen Jessica in a while and, before he could protest any further, I hung up.

The shocking thing is that I was actually telling the truth. Jessica didn't knock on my door until after I'd hung up on her husband. When she stepped into my apartment, I started, "Zac just called—" She cut me off by wrapping her arms around my back, pulling my suddenly compliant body close to hers, and kissing my lips. Weakly, I tried to kiss back but there was something new about her; an aggression that let me know that she was here to kiss me and not vice versa.

Finally, she released me and stared not at me but instead at the blank walls behind me.

Staring back at her, I managed to find my voice long enough to say, "Uh—hello."

"Who am I?" she asked. Her voice had strange tone to it, an almost ethereal sound. Looking back on it, she seemed almost to be just a shade of Jessica, floating through my reality as if she had secretly sprung from my dreams.

"You're Jessica," I said.

"And who's that?"

"You."

She continued to stare straight through me. I felt like a shallow oasis, drying up under the desert sun.

Again, she spoke, "If you had to introduce me to someone, what would you say? How would you explain who I am?"

"I don't know," This was getting frustrated and I really wanted a nice, cold beer. "This is Jessica Evans, my ex-girlfriend and eternal muse."

A mirthless smile – the first smile I'd seen from her in quite some time – twisted onto her face. "That's what I thought," she said.

Now, her tone was one of judgement and disappointment. This had been a test and obviously, I'd managed to fail. She turned around, opened the door, and stepped outside.

"Jessica, wait—" I said as I started to step forward.

She looked back at me and then closed my own front door in my face. Outside, I could hear her walking away but for some reason, I didn't follow. No, that's my romanticizing the whole incident. It wasn't for some reason that I didn't reason. It was for one very specific reason; I could either follow Jessica in an effort to pass whatever test her whims had designed for me or I could drink a nonjudgmental, predictable beer. I chose the beer.

There are rumors about what Jessica did for the rest of that night. Some say they saw her acting pretty stoned at the End of the World. Others claim she ended up having a one-night stand with some random frat boy, something that I chose to doubt. Everyone agrees that whenever she ran into a friend or even a casual acquaintance, she would ask them what they thought of when they heard the name Jessica Evans. Just about everyone said they either thought of my ex-girlfriend or Zac's wife.

The next morning, to her husband she returned. He'd spent the night waiting for her and as soon as he saw her, he demanded to know where she'd been. Much later, Zac told me her reply.

"I was meeting the common people."

"And, man," Zac said in a slurred voice (Did I mention we were both rather drunk at the time?), "her tone could have melted acid."

Melted acid. It was the type of phrase that would have inspired my old creative writing professor to scribble, "What does this mean?" off in the margins. The phrase didn't make any sense but for some reason, it was appropriate and I certainly wasn't going to call Zac on it. Sometimes, things just don't make sense. Sometimes, they just happen.

14) Howl

For the next few weeks, Jessica continued to disappear only to return home in the early morning hours. She stopped going to her classes, eventually missing so many days that she was withdrawn from the university. Zac, hard at work on his Master's, was the one who had to deal with the snooty ladies in administration who call to say Jessica was no longer a good student. When Jessica wandered into their apartment, this time obviously drunk, Zac was waiting for her. He said she was making him look bad. He was losing credibility with the English Department because of her.

I'm proud to say that Jessica didn't say a word. She just lay down on their couch and fell asleep. Zac responded by going into their bedroom and falling asleep himself. When he woke up, he discovered that Jessica was already up and using his electric razor to shave off her hair.

Zac stared as clumps of her hair tumbled down to the floor. Finally, he managed to sputter, "Jessica, what the Hell are you doing?"

"I'm changing myself," she replied, nonchalantly, "I'm doing it for you. If your wife is such an embarrassment then maybe I should be someone else."

Freshly bald, Jessica left their apartment and Zac wasn't surprised when she didn't return that day. Or the next day. Or for the entire week. Instead, he just sat by the phone waiting for her to call. Her voice, he knew, would be back to the sweet, girlish voice that he had fallen in love with. He imagined she'd be crying, having realized her mistakes. He'd take her back, get her the right help, and everything could get back to normal.

Jessica never called.

Finally, her credit card bill arrived at the apartment. When

Zac opened it, he discovered she had charged over three hundred dollars to Greyhound. Charges had been made across the southwest and the latest ones were in Denver.

He called me and asked if I would come to Denver with him. "If Jessica won't talk to me," he said, "maybe she'll talk to you." After getting him to agree to cover my expenses, I agreed. (I understand the majority of the checks he wrote while on his quest have since bounced. Ah, the scourge that is money.)

We drove to Denver in his red Mercedes and along the way, he talked and I drank. He couldn't understand why Jessica was doing this. "She's acting like I've betrayed her, like I did something wrong!" he kept repeating like a mantra of self-pity. He told me about their fights, about his father's funeral, about how they used to ride Greyhound because that's what the common people did. Myself, I was mostly speechless. My mind, to be honest, was reeling and not just from the booze. Jessica was missing and here I was, with her husband, driving to Colorado in a red Mercedes to save her. It was like one of those movies that turned me off the '60s or that Zac refused to watch. ("Movies are just an opiate designed to make us blind to reality," he told me – yes, he actually talked like this at times.) It was strange; Zac had been a major part of my life but this was the first time I'd ever truly tried to know him as something other than a shadowy nuisance. I quickly discovered that most of my suspicions were correct. Zac was a pretentious fool. If he'd been some guy I'd met in a bar, I'd probably try to pick a fight with him. However, at that one, twisted moment, we were both just two guys who desperately wanted to find a girl. I wanted to find my ex-girlfriend Jessica Adams and Zac was searching for his wife Jessica Evans but what mattered was that we both needed Jessica.

Our Jessica.

In Denver, we went to a coffeehouse where Jessica had used her credit card several times. The Hangman's Knot was almost identical to BPU's The End of the World; something I pointed out as we stepped through the front doors but which Zac failed to hear.

He scanned the crowd of aging hippies and neo-beatniks. "Do you see her?"

I shook my head, "No."

We both had brought a picture of Jessica and we circulated through the Hangman's Knot, asking if anyone had seen her. Unfortunately, my picture featured Jessica as a 18 year-old, fresh-faced college girl with a thick lion's mane of hair. Zac's picture was more recent and showed a serious-looking, attractive woman with a professionally cropped haircut. Neither of us had a picture of the enigma who had fled to Denver.

Finally, one thin man with a goat-tee looked at both of our pictures and said, "Yeah, I know her."

"Do you know where she is?" Zac asked, his voice suddenly rushed.

The thin man took a slow sip from his espresso, obviously enjoying the knowledge that he held our emotions in the palm of his aesthetic hand. Finally, he said with a slight smirk, "She's gone."

Zac's voice sounded as if it were about to break. "What? Gone where?"

"She hung out for a while," the thin man shrugged, "and then she said she had to go. She didn't say where but I didn't really ask. She said she wanted to watch the trains go by or something."

Zac crumpled his hand into a fist, crushing his wife's face in his palm. He turned around and, shoulders stooped, walked out of the coffeehouse.

The thin man looked over at me and said, "You guys cops or something?"

"No," I shook my head, "He's a Marxist and I'm a drunk."

"Cool," He seemed reasonably impressed. Stroking his goat-tee, he continued, "Jesus, man, that girl was fucked up."

"Happens to the best of us."

"But, hey, she gave great head!" He erupted into a high pitched squeal of a laugh.

I stared at him as he joyfully rocked in his seat, espresso in hand. For all I knew, he was lying but just hearing him say that – just the possibility that my Jessica, Zac's Jessica, had been with this guy, this stranger – I wanted to punch him. I wanted to knock that obnoxious sneer right off his goddamn face.

Instead, painfully aware that I was not a brawler, I turned my back to his giggles and I walked out of the coffeehouse. As I stepped out onto the street, I saw Zac pulling up in the Mercedes. Impatiently, he motioned for me to get in and I thought about the man laughing.

"One minute," I said before turning around, walking back into the coffeehouse, and sucker punching the goat-tee guy. No longer laughing, he fell back out of his chair and to the floor. As his espresso spilled out across the hardwood, I ran out of the coffeehouse. Cowardly actions, I know, but they still provided the only satisfaction I got from our trip to Denver.

15) Greyhound In Passing

As Zac insisted, we visited everywhere else in Denver that Jessica had used her credit card and, except for the thin, goat-tee guy, nobody remembered her from our pictures. As Zac grew more and more frustrated, I pointed out, "They probably just don't recognize her with hair."

To this, Zac replied, "I'm never leaving Denver. I'm staying here until I find her."

Hearing the steadfastly naïve conviction in his voice, I actually felt sorry for him. Jessica, his wife, had left him, probably cheated on him, and he was still willing to believe he could search forever. Staring at him, I realized that, whereas I lusted for Jessica only as a teenage wet dream, Zac was desperately looking for the woman he loved. Whether he had driven her away or not, he was, at least, sincere.

He was also allowing his life to collapse around him and I

said, trying to keep my voice cold and practical, "Zac, she's not in Denver anymore. She's gone."

"Then where is she!?"

I sighed and repeated "She's gone."

The next morning, we started to drive back to BPU. On the highway, Zac again told me he was going to keep looking. Every moment he could afford, he was going to look for her.

"You're welcome to come with me," Zac said, "because you're an important part of her life, of who she is."

I smiled even as my mind wondered just who exactly that was.

"But," Zac continued, "she's my wife. And if she decides to come back home, she's coming with me. Understand?"

Before I could answer, a Greyhound bus passed the Mercedes. Both of us looked up at the bus and, though neither said it, we were hoping to see Jessica staring back through one of the windows. Instead, we just saw a collection of strangers and as the bus went past us, their faces blurred into one anonymous mass.

16) Apocalypse

As a human being, I always want things to end with a bang, with a neat act of melodrama that wraps everything up. As a writer, I know it can't. Zac still looks for Jessica and sometimes, I go with him and most times, I don't. I still don't think highly of him but his search for Jessica remains strangely pure. He swears to me that he's not going to try to make her come back. He says he just wants a chance to understand and for some reason, I believe him. I don't consider Zac Evans to be much of a man but as a human being, I am sometimes envious.

Of course, there are many things that we know but choose not to discuss. We didn't know Jessica and one reason she was able to disappear so effectively is because we only understood her as an ex-girlfriend or as a wife. Now that she's neither of those things, we probably wouldn't recognize her if she was sitting across the room from us. For all I know, she could be reading this right now and smirking at what a self-congratulatory mess I've turned her escape into. I think a lot about what Jake Ballard once said – "too much to prove." We expected Jessica to prove she was worthy of us and once we failed her, she had to prove something to herself. What I can't pinpoint beyond grand concepts of freedom and part of me curses myself for not bothering to ask when I could.

Its nearly 7:10 in the morning and I've been writing for four hours. My love will be waking soon and I'll be going to sleep. And some nights, she'll look at me and there will be some wayward emotion in my eyes that I can't explain. Sometimes, it will be Zac and Jessica. Sometimes, it will be something else.

But, we'll go on.

Because in the end, what else can you do?

JULY 30TH, 1999

Saw a flyer this afternoon saying that Joe Criswell was going to be showing his films at the Underground Theatre later tonight and, out of *ennui* and Jessica-centered depression, I attended. All the elite members of the Dallas, Texas arts scene were there and it was disturbing how many of them knew me and found the time to remember their favorite "crazy old Charlie" stories. Can't figure out why I'm so popular but I know it bugs the Hell out of me. I'm a lovable eccentric now. *Sarcasm Boy*: Everyone's difficult drinking buddy! J.C. arrived an hour late. Wearing the exact same clothes, J.C. gave the exact same speech he gave four years ago in Longmont and I swear to Christ, I think the exact same people applauded. Conclusion: Its time to vanish before I start clapping too.

ENLIGHTENMENT

They stood there, consumed with excited conversation, waiting and waiting. As the minutes became hours, some started to wonder if this was some sort of cruel joke, another sign of Peter's sense of humor. They were quickly shushed. It was not good to speak such words in front of Peter's Gate.

And then they saw it.

In a blaze of fire came a golden chariot pulled by a fleet of powerful horses. As their hooves hit the street, diamonds flew into the beautifully clean air and as the chariot came closer, they could all hear the sounds of an angelic choir singing the praises of their gatekeeper. What a glorious sight it was but for the assembled crowd, it was nothing special. Oh, maybe all that pomp had impressed them when they first arrived but by now, they'd seen it too many times to be impressed. Heavenly choir or not, Peter was late.

And over to the side, expressionless, Bill Shakespeare watched them all.

The crowd parted to let the chariot through, remembering with an uneasy air what had happened during Adlai Stevenson's first week. Ol' Adlai had spent too much time wandering around in a daze and muttering that he was in the wrong place. "I didn't even believe in this stuff!" he kept repeating. Preoccupied, he didn't even notice the chariot baring down on him until the horses were literally pounding their hooves across his bald head. Of course, it wasn't that big of a thing. Pain, injury, death – those were all distant memories. No, what had been frightening had been the ringing out Adlai got from Peter. "This isn't the Ivy League, professor!" Peter had yelled and poor Adlai looked like he was on the verge of tears. Significantly, Adlai had turned down all offers to join the crowd at the gates. "Enlightenment?" he had scoffed to Will Rogers, "What do I need with enlightenment? I learned everything I needed to know before I even got here!" (Later Rogers would tell Billy Sunday, "I never met a man I didn't like. Then I met Adlai Stevenson.")

Peter, wearing that black Armani suit that he wore only when he absolutely had to, apologized for being late as he disembarked from the chariot. He explained that he'd been fishing. "That's what I usually do on my day off," he said, "I figured I might as well have at least half of my day for myself. Is that okay, folks?" Nervously, the crowd said yes, of course, that was okay. Peter's voice boomed as he continued, "All right, folks, we all know why we're all here and its not the pleasure of my company, is it? Let's get on with it. I've got fish to skin"

And the crowd erupted into questions. ("No," Peter would later correct Lew Wallace, "not questions. Demands. They were demanding their answers. Ungrateful infidel dogs.") Never before had the jewel-encrusted city heard such a commotion and as he listened, Peter swore to himself that it would never be heard again.

"Who killed John F. Kennedy!?" A popular one; several asked it. Some expected to hear the Mafia, some the military-industrial complex, at least one blamed Dean Acheson.

"Jack the Ripper! Give me the name!" Conan Doyle practically jumped up and down, waving his arms in desperation.

"Deep Throat!? WHO WAS DEEP THROAT!?" Ed Muskie's tearful voice cut through the air like a rapier.

Beside him, Richard Nixon – usually just happy to actually be there – vigorously nodded his jowly face and gutturally added, "Yeah – who was that <expletive deleted>?"

"The Lindbergh baby! Who kidnapped the Lindbergh baby!? Was it the housekeeper!?"

"Jimmy Hoffa!? Where is he?" ("Where do you think?" someone was heard to reply as he pointed downward, proof that even then humor survived.)

"What about Marilyn Monroe!?" Paul Lynde literally stamped his foot, furiously feeling ignored even still, "Was it that Peter Lawford!?"

"How about Judge Crater!? Was it the Mafia!?"

"Did the studios have Thelma Todd murdered!?"

"Who shot Huey Newton? What white boy did it!?"

"Abbie Hoffman! That wasn't no suicide!"

"Vince Foster," a new timer demanded, "did the CIA have him shot!?"

"Warren Harding!" an old timer who had been waiting an eternity wanted to know, "Did the Duchess really poison him!?"

And over to the side, expressionless, Bill Shakespeare watched them all.

Peter walked through the crowd, from person to person. He nodded as he listened to every question and he searched his mind for the name of every murderer and conspirator in the history of the world. Gruffly, he told each person who was responsible for what. He did so with a tight expression on his battle-lined face, trying to keep his volcanic temper from erupting. *I was called the Rock,* he thought, *The Rock on Which All This Was Built. I was tortured, I saw my brothers murdered, my best friends stoned to death, and I gave my life. I hung upside down on a cross and I did it all without needing answers. I did it all so these people could come up here and demand to know who shot their Presidents.* He wanted to tell them they were a bunch of ungrateful fools who wouldn't have survived ten minutes back in Galilee. He wanted to know why, with paradise gleaming before them, these trivial mysteries still mattered. But Peter followed orders; such was his faith. Keeping his emotions to himself, Peter carefully spelled out each name, explained each motive, and told the curious where they might find the guilty.

When everyone had been spoken to, Peter looked over the crestfallen crowd and asked, "That it?"

Nobody said a word but instead stared down at the shimmering ground. Finally, from the side, an English-accented thespian voice sang out, "That is all."

Peter nodded, "All right then. I've got fish to take care of."

And in a blaze of fire, Peter's chariot was gone. The crowd stood quietly for a few minutes. They milled around the gates without direction or purpose. It was a former U.S. congressman who finally spoke up.

"Who the Hell's—" and here he said the unknown name of the man who killed JFK, "I've never even heard of the guy before! And I read every book there was!"

"What about Jack the Ripper!?" Conan Doyle agreed, "I can't even remember that so-called *name* Peter gave me!"

The others in the crowd agreed. They'd been patient, as had been asked. They'd shown up at the agreed upon time and they'd asked their questions. They'd waited to hear Peter's answers and they'd accepted the names without argument but now – now that they had their answers, they were ticked off. Who were these people that Peter mentioned? These people who were responsible for the crimes that had defined the crowd's lives for so many years? Strangers; men nobody else had ever heard of. This seemed somehow unfair. Everyone read Conan Doyle and yet his mind had been dominated by – ah, Hell, he couldn't even remember the bloody name! The crowd hadn't gathered to hear yet more new names. They'd gathered to find out that what they'd always suspected was right. "The truth," Tolstoy later explained, "has nothing to do with it!"

And seeing the crowd's discontent, Bill Shakespeare finally walked toward them.

"My friends!" he shouted in a voice that still belonged to the theater, "My friends! I ask for just one second of your time! Lend me your ears for just one second!"

Slowly, a silence descended over the crowd and they turned to face this handsome, always smartly dressed figure. Though friendly enough, he often seemed to hold himself just a bit above the rest of them.

"Now Peter has spoken to us," Shakespeare continued, "and certainly Peter is an honorable man! We have asked Peter our questions and he has given us the answers as he knows them to be! And we are not happy with those answers are we!?"

The crowd, energized to hear their discontent expressed in one solid voice, agreed.

"But Peter is an honorable man. On that we are all agreed. But let us say, just for one second as an open-minded people which we most surely are, let us just ask one more question. From where does Peter get his answers? For Peter is an honorable man but he is not one to question his leaders. That we all know. For Peter is a man with no understanding of the rest us, yet he remains an honorable man! So let me ask you one last time, where does Peter get his answers and why do they give him those answers? When we can answer that, then we will have true enlightenment! So, I ask thricefold, where does Peter get his answers?"

And the crowd, its paranoia healthily restored, stood at the Gates of Paradise and wondered where well meaning but oh-so innocent Peter had gotten the answers he'd so effortlessly reeled out. As their questions grew into a bubbling mass of confusion, Bill Shakespeare allowed himself to smile. He could feel it. The crowd looked to him to be its new prophet and as they begged him to confirm their fearful obsessions, expressionless he was no longer.

SEPTEMBER 11TH, 2001

As I write this, New York is still on fire. I worked the overnight shift and I really should be asleep but I'm afraid of what might happen if I close my eyes. I'm scared of what I'll discover once I wake up. It started when I got home from work this morning. I checked my e-mail and found a note from one of the news services that I subscribe to. The note read: "Due to terrorist attacks, news will be delayed today." It's a conservative news service so I assumed that some left-wing computer hackers had maybe been playing havoc with the sight. Then Connie called me from the school where she teaches and she asked me if I was watching the news. She told me the World Trade Center had collapsed, the Pentagon had collapsed, the Capitol had been blown up, and that nobody knew what was happening. She told me to stay inside and be careful. My Dad had been supposed to be on a plane today, going on a business trip. That trip's been cancelled and I thank God that we all know where our loved ones are. After I got off the phone, I turned on the TV and there it was. That damn footage – an airplane flying into one of the Trade Center towers and the huge fireball exploding from the side of the building. I watch this with a sickened feeling. I see footage of bodies falling from the flaming buildings and then, again and again, the towers collapsing on top of people vainly fleeing. I keep watching because I keep hoping to hear that this is some sort of mistake. I know that's not true but I watch in vain hope. Images of death; that's all I can find. They say 50,000 people might be dead. They're in New York and I'm in Dallas but I feel like I've lost my best friends as I watch their deaths repeated again and again. Its obscene really – these innocents will now only be known for the way they died. The more the image plays, the more they stop being human but become instead props in some horrible melodrama that we can't escape. Finally, after eleven hours of this, I couldn't take anymore. I had to escape. So I ran down the street to Barnes and Noble and spent an hour raiding the humor section; reading everything in an attempt to remember what it was like to laugh. The store is nearly deserted and the few people there are silent. What can one say? I leave at ten when they close the store. As I walk across the parking lot, a woman runs up to me. She's tall and very thin with dirty blonde hair and a pretty face that is crisscrossed with age lines even though I don't think she's even close to being my age. She tells me that she's looking for a street. She's been walking for hours and she has to meet her friends at a particular house on a particular street but she can't find the street. She's desperate. She tells me, "I don't know where I'm going." I smile back at her and say, "Neither do I." And in the most selfish of ways, admitting that brings me some ill-earned peace. I don't know where I'm going but I know where I am and in the end, what else can any of us ask for?

THOUGHTS AFTER A POEM

As I lay my pen down to rest
I stare down at these words
And I'm not sure what is true
And what is false
And I'm not sure what I wrote
And what I stole

ACKNOWLEDGEMENTS

This book is dedicated, as promised, to AJF
Many of these stories previously appeared in much different versions.

Jeffrey's Spoken originally appeared in *Jack the Daw* (Jeffrey Ellis, editor)

The Vile Perfume of Blazing Bread, Blazing Plain Woman, and *The Last Roundtable* all originally appeared in *Poetic Expressions* (Gail Shrader, editor)

How I Let Allen Ginsberg Beat Me Off appeared in *Maverick Press* (Carol Cullar, editor)

Mowing the Lawn and *Coyotes Don't Scream* both originally appeared in *Dream International Quarterly* (Charles "Chuck" Jones, editor)

Myself, the Girl, and the Bastard from Brazil appeared in *Ebbing Tide* (Pat Sammis, Ed.)

A Night in the Life of Warren Aackland and *Venus Rising* both originally appeared in *The Pages of Babel* (Matthew Talmadge Raymond, editor)

Looking for Armenia, Goin' South, and *12 Midnight Bruce Hall Lobby University of North Texas* all originally appeared in *Parallax* (Jonathan Bell, editor)

Enlightenment originally appeared in *Pendragon* (Elizabeth Hyman, editor)

Thoughts After A Poem originally appeared in *Sophomore Jinx*

Criswell was Right and *Two Car Collision on Highway 61* both began life as performance pieces and both were first brought to life by the National Organic Theater (N.O.T.) in a December,

1996 performance at Richland Community College in Dallas, Texas. They were performed by Jeff Ellis, Jonathan Bell, J. Lea Weaver, and Heather Hinds.